# George Burns

## IN HIS OWN WORDS

# George Burns

## IN HIS OWN WORDS

Compiled and Edited by
HERB FAGEN

Carroll & Graf Publishers, Inc.
New York

*Carroll & Graf Publishers, Inc.*
*260 Fifth Avenue*
*New York, NY 10001*

*ISBN 0-7867-0352-0*

*Library of Congress Cataloging-in-Publication Data are available.*

*Manufactured in the United States of America.*

To my Aunt Edith

# Acknowledgments

My deep appreciation to the Museum of Television and Radio in Beverly Hills, California, for access to their vast library collection of radio and TV shows. The same appreciation to Cary O'Dell of the Museum of Broadcast Communication in Chicago, for again extending his services and resources to this project.

My great thanks to Roy Leonard, the Tribune Company, Chicago, Illinois, and WGN Radio for permission to include segments of Roy Leonard's 1980 interview with George Burns; to CBS for allowing me to use segments of Ed Bradley's interview with George Burns in a 1988 segment of *60 Minutes;* and to Karen Corbin at Tribune Entertainment in Los Angeles for permission to use a segment of a Joan Rivers interview with George Burns.

My thanks also to my agent, Jake Elwell of Wieser & Wieser, for getting this project off the ground, and to Herman Graf of Carroll & Graf Publishers, Inc., for the opportunity of allowing me to put this project together. To Gert Fagen and the Phillips family, my grateful appreciation for your continued support.

Deep thanks to Chuck Schaden and Don Visovatti of *Metre Golden Memories* in Chicago, and Ira Kramer at *Movie Star News* in New York, for supplying the splendid array of photographs which appear in this book.

—*Herb Fagen*
*Walnut Creek, California, 1996*

# Contents

# Introduction

He was a pearl of wisdom, wit, humor, and decency. His life spanned vaudeville, radio, stage, film screen, and television. He was the unorthodox son of Orthodox Jewish parents who taught us all how to be forever young. With the passing of George Burns at age 100, the pages closed on a unique biography, the life of a man endearing in quality and enduring of stature.

He was born Nathan Birnbaum on the Lower East Side of New York when William McKinley was president, and before the Spanish-American War had begun. The Wright Brothers had yet to launch a flight; there would not be a World Series for another seven years; and the czars still ruled Russia.

George Burns' career spanned every conceivable form of entertainment. In 1910, he was just another kid trying to break into vaudeville. "I was a terrible singer and a terrible dancer," he once admitted. "By the time I realized I had no talent, I was a big success." He began in the early days of radio with Gracie, then conquered television with eight seasons of *The Burns and Allen Show*. He became an Oscar winner at age 79 with *The Sunshine Boys* in 1975, and then a box-office mainstay with *Oh, God!* and two sequels. Did he ever think of retiring? Not in his lifetime, he would joke. "I'm going to stay in show business until I'm the only one left."

Decades of audiences remember Burns' distinctive voice. According to Burns it ran in the family. "My father was a wonderful man, a very religious man,"

George once recalled. "During the High Holidays if the cantor caught colds and couldn't sing, my father would take his place. One year it happened. The cantor got sick, so my father did the singing. The following year the same cantor got sick. Instead of sending for my father, they closed the synagogue. I think I inherited my voice from my father."

And with that voice George Burns would thrill millions and millions of people the world over, as the cigar-puffing comedian of caustic wit, often the victim of Gracie Allen's harebrained ideas on both radio and TV.

After appearing for three years in vaudeville, George Burns and Gracie Allen were married in Cleveland on January 7, 1926. On February 15, 1932, Burns and Allen gave their first performance on their own radio show. During almost twenty years on radio, they attracted an audience estimated at more than forty-five million listeners. "[Gracie] banks sincerity against a wild joke, and that's what makes it funny," said George. "If somebody asks what time it is and Gracie says, 'Look on the floor, maybe it fell down,' she's got to say it as if she meant it, or it won't go at all."

George always considered himself an "expert" on the good old days. "After all," he'd insist, "I was there. There were no automobiles, no television, no radio, no refrigerators, electric ovens, or pop toasters. And if they had been invented, I wouldn't have had them anyway, because as far as my family was concerned money hadn't been invented either."

George loved Gracie dearly. She was his light and his inspiration, his wife and his partner. But he did have some problems with Gracie's family. "Gracie had a nephew," George once recalled. "One day he had a terrible cold and went to the doctor. The doctor told him to take something warm, so he took the doctor's over-coat."

George never wavered in his praise for Gracie. Like he said, he lied a lot. But never when it came to Gracie. He was often asked about his greatest asset as a performer. He never hesitated to reply, "I was married to her for thirty-eight years."

When their thirty-eight-year marriage ended with Gracie's death in 1964, George Burns packaged his trademark cigar, surrounded himself with lovely young ladies, and marketed a new career. "Happiness is your mistress coming down with morning sickness, then finding out it's only from some bad sausage," he said, puffing away slyly on his El Producto cigar.

George also knew the secret of how to keep a wife happy. "Surprise her with a sweater two sizes too small. She'll be flattered, she'll love you for it, and since she can't wear it, you can give it back to your secretary."

No matter where he was, George Burns was never at a loss for words. His lifetime spanned sixteen American presidents. "Personally, I've always liked Ronald Reagan, and I think he's made a great president. In fact, I think he's the best president the Screen Actors Guild ever had."

Yes, George Burns had a story for every occasion and an amusing thought for every milestone—a hundred years of stories, thoughts, anecdotes, and songs. Irreverent, sentimental, serious, sweet, and bittersweet, George Burns didn't have all the answers, but he sure gave us some pretty good ones.

The whole world will miss him.

He was born with a gift of laughter
and a sense that the world was mad.

—Raphael Sabatini, *Scaramouche*

# George Burns
## IN HIS OWN WORDS

# CHAPTER ONE

# Nathan Birnbaum

*"All my stories are basically honest.*
*But from then on you're in show business."*
—Cited in *Time* (August 6, 1979)

William McKinley was president of the United States when the future George Burns entered the world on January 20, 1896. His parents, Dora and Louis, were Orthodox Jews who had immigrated to New York from Eastern Europe and had settled on the Lower East Side of New York. Nathan was the ninth of twelve children, seven girls and five boys. To say that the family was poor would be an understatement.

Part of what made George Burns so funny was his ironic and self-deprecating attitude about himself and life in general. Here he tells Dotson Rader of *Esquire* about his humble beginnings.

"I was born on Pitt Street on the Lower East Side in New York. We were very very poor, only we didn't know it. And the fact was that the *toilets* were in the *yard,* see, down three flights of stairs. By the time you got there you didn't have to go to the toilet anymore. Because it was a hell of a long walk. . . . They had gaslights, but the upstairs halls were dark. So if you had to go to the bathroom at night in the wintertime, my sisters were scared stiff.

"We weren't very brave either. So my mother used to talk them to the bathroom downstairs. She'd open up the window and shout down to them. So when my sisters went to the toilet they knew it in Altoona. Because you could hear my mother all over town."

"I had seven sisters and four brothers. Twelve in the family. We were dirt poor. We ate one of my sisters. Everybody had big families in the neighborhood. It doesn't mean that the Jews were great lovers. It meant that it was freezing down there.

"When my mother and father got married, my mother wanted to go to work, but my father put his foot down and said, 'No, dear. I will not allow it!' So my mother stayed home and raised twelve children and did all the washing, cooking, and scrubbing. My father was a gentleman of the old school. He didn't think a wife should work."

"I started in show business when I was five. I used to dance and hang around with the neighborhood organ grinder. The people clapped for me. But when my father died I was forced to go into show business for real. My father was a deeply religious man, but he died when I was seven. . . . Yes, I think I'm a religious person but that's between God and myself. You notice I give him top billing."

Louis Birnbaum, George's father, died of influenza during the epidemic of 1904. He was forty-seven years old. George's mother, Dora, was forty-three and alone. She had twelve children, the youngest of whom was six months old.

"My mother had a great sense of humor. She never

took life too seriously. But my father made up for it. He was an Orthodox Jew and felt he was just marking time in this world. . . . The only jobs he ever had were concerned with the temple, teaching children how to pray or making sure the food was strictly kosher at somebody's wedding."

When her husband died, Mrs. Birnbaum went to work in the garment industry. To help make ends meet, George hustled the streets, shining shoes, selling newspapers, and running errands.

"I've always hustled. It seems that everything I did always had a touch of show business in it. I remember going up and down the streets singing, selling crackers. I'd buy a box of crackers for two cents. I'd sell them in groups of three and end up making a penny profit on each box."

Then he went to work at Rosenzweig's candy store on the corner of Columbia Street and Stanton. It would be the start of The Pee Wee Quartet, and his foray into show business.

"Four of us kids used to work at a candy store. We used to make syrup, like strawberry, chocolate, and vanilla. There was a letter carrier named Lou Farley, who loved harmony singing. He just wanted the whole world to whistle harmony. When he'd whistle, you'd just come down and get your mail, and when you got there he'd teach you harmony singing. We didn't know we could sing, but we sang."

Mr. Rosenzweig allowed the boys to sing regularly in his cellar. The lead singer was a boy named Moishe Friedman, whom they called Toda. In those days Nathan had a pleasant tenor voice. Together with Mortzy (the baritone) and Heshy (the bass), they formed The Pee Wee Quartet.

"One day we were making syrup and we looked up—because we were in the basement—and there were six or seven people standing upstairs listening to us. And they threw a few pennies at us. I said, 'This is a business we gotta get in. We can make more at that than mixing chocolate.' So that's how we got together. We sang on ferryboats and on streetcars, yachts, and saloons, and we passed around the hat. *Sometimes they stole the hat.* . . . So when I was eight years old I was already in show business."

It was not that unusual back then for young boys to harmonize. Such routines were popular in vaudeville. The five Marx Brothers were already performing with their mother and calling themselves "The Six Musical Mascots." But things weren't always easy for George and The Pee Wee Quartet.

He told many stories about The Pee Wee Quartet over the years, always with that inimical deprecating sense of humor of his. Shortly after sustaining a stroke in 1995, he was still able to relate this one to his speech therapist.

"When I was eight years old, I sang in The Pee Wee Quartet and we worked at this Presbyterian church. And I got an Ingersoll watch. I went home and I said, 'Ma, I've been a Jew for eight years and I never got anything. I was a Presbyterian for one day and I got a watch.' My mother said, 'Help me hang the wash!' Three days later the watch stopped. I became a Jew again."

In an interview with Roy Leonard of WGN Radio in Chicago, he talked about the perils of the four Jewish boys singing in a Gentile neighborhood.

"I'll tell you a cute story. We were singing on Halloween. We came from a Jewish neighborhood on the Lower East Side. On Halloween we went into the Gentile neighborhood to sing and we made eighteen dollars, which was a fortune. We might have made two or three dollars, but eighteen, never.

"So when we came out there were a lot of kids dressed up. They saw us making this money and wanted to take it from us. So the four of us ran. We kept running and running and running, until we got to 10th Street and Avenue C, which is the Jewish Boys Club. And we went into the club and said, 'Look, we made eighteen dollars and these little Gentile kids are trying to take it away from us.' They said, 'You stay right here and we'll go and chase them away.' So they went and chased them away, and they came back and they took our eighteen dollars and chased us home."

In those days many kids dropped out of school by the time they were ten to help support their families. Lou Farley arranged for the boys to sing at an amateur contest in the local movie house. They won a five-dollar prize.

"I dropped out of school when I was in the fourth grade. I played hooky. That's how I got out of school. They were glad I left school. See, I read in the paper that Caruso used to eat a lot of garlic. So when I played hooky from school, my teacher wrote a letter of thanks to my mother.

"Oh, my mother was very funny. I brought a girl home once. I was fourteen years old and she was sixteen. And she wore lipstick. In those days if you wore lipstick you were a prostitute. She not only had lipstick on, she had a beauty mark. I said to my mother, 'I want you to meet my sweetheart, Greta.' She said, 'Are you Jewish?' Greta said, 'No!' 'Do you understand Jewish?' my mother said. Greta said, 'No!' My mother turned around and said some Yiddish words which meant 'go to hell!' Then she turns around and says to Greta, 'I just told my son what a charming girl you are.'

"I came home once and they were having breakfast. I was the bad one in the family. She said, 'Natty, all your seven sisters married virgins.' I said, 'Mama, the reason they married virgins was because they weren't very pretty.' My mother said, 'Pass the salt.' My mother thought that I was going to be a gangster."

Nathan quit The Pee Wee Quartet and became half of a dance act with a fellow named Abie Kaplan. Abie taught Nathan to dance. It was called the time step, a basic tap-dancing combination, and the two youths would practice by dancing down the street. It was then that Nathan Birnbaum became George Burns.

We cannot be entirely sure as to how he chose his stage name. One explanation suggests that "Burns" came from a shortening of Birnbaum. But according to George there was another reason, which makes for a far more interesting story.

"We would steal coal from the Burns Brothers Coal Yard to help heat our mothers' kitchens. We loaded up our baggy knickers with chunks of coal. So the kids in the neighborhood began calling us 'the Burns Brothers.'

"We were five brothers and we all loved our brother George. He hated the name Izzy and changed it to George. I loved my brother Izzy and if George was good enough for him, it was good enough for me."

Burns' fancy footwork turned him into a dance instructor at an early age. "That's the way I made my living. I had two dancing studios when I was fourteen. It was Bernstein and Burns. We called ourselves B.B's College of Dancing. We taught the waltz, the two-step and the fox trot. The funny thing is when I used to teach these fellows how to dance, I played the part of a girl when I danced with them. The problem was they couldn't dance with anybody but me. So whenever they went to a wedding I had to go with them."

"We got most of our clients right off the immigration boats at Ellis Island. We told them the first requirement of being a United States citizen was a five-dollar course of dancing lessons. Dishonest, you say! Maybe. But have you ever been hungry?"

# CHAPTER TWO

# Vaudeville

*"I've already told you I lie a lot.*
*But believe me, I was awful.*
*If I was going to make up something,*
*I'd tell you I was good.*
*But even I'm not that big a liar."*
—Interview with Roy Leonard, WGN Radio (1980)

As young as he was, George Burns knew he was in show business. The jobs may have been scarce, but he was in love with a dream. He also had to work to help his mother and things were far from easy.

"I would have sold *The Saturday Evening Post,* but Ben Franklin hadn't started to publish it yet. I was a kid, but already an old man. Why? I didn't have a job in show business. I was in show business but I wasn't working. I had makeup, I had music, I had pictures, but I had no job. But I was in love with what I was doing.

"I'd walk to Hammerstein's from Second Avenue to 42nd Street and Broadway to save five cents. Right next door to Hammerstein's was the Putman Building, and all the theater managers had their offices there. So I'd ride up and down the elevator with a cigar in my mouth and my picture in one hand and my music under the other, hoping that someone would give me a job. And one day the elevator boy says to me, 'Kid, don't you work any other place but this elevator?'

"I'd go to the Automat, you know. I had one of my sister's hairpins. And I'd stand by the beef stew, which was the most expensive dish they had then. It was fifteen cents. And when somebody put in money and took out the beef stew from the cubicle, I'd put a hairpin in there so the door wouldn't close. Then I got beef stew for nothing. I even sold fifteen-cent beef stews for ten cents at the Automat. That's a good profit on nothing. I'd manage, you know.

"I'd go into one of those places where they would press your suit while you stood in your underwear. I'd put the suit on hot—I wouldn't bend my knees until it had cooled off—and walk down the street with a cigar in my mouth. Nobody asked me what I did for a living. They knew it. I was in show business.

"I'd go to the theater under one name and get fired after the first show. In a week or two, I'd be back in the same fleabag with a different name and in blackface. But I'd rather be a flop in a business I love, than a success in felt hats. All I wanted was to be in show business."

George always wore that newly pressed suit to his auditions. An impressive front was most important for an entertainer. More often than not as he walked stiffly down the street, some wise guy would yell, "Going to an audition?" Auditions taught him promptness, a key factor for a young entertainer on the move. He took it seriously.

"In vaudeville, you came in on the first morning and got a check for number one, number two, number three, and so on. Whoever got rehearsal check number one got to sing his first choice.

"See, there were only three or four great songs, for instance, 'You Made Me Love You.' Everybody sang the same four songs. But if you were first, you got the number one check—you got to sing it.

"From eight to twenty-seven I did all kinds of lousy acts. I worked with a seal. I worked with a dog. I worked with another fellow. All bad acts. But in those days there were theaters you could be bad in. There's no place to be bad today. The kids have to do *The Comedy Store* or *The Johnny Carson Show*. I loved what I was doing. [But] I was sorry for the audience."

George summarizes his early years of show business frustration in a 1977 interview for *Macleans* magazine.

"I had to change my name so often because nobody who knew who I was would ever have me back again. Of course, if I had any sense, I would have changed my act, not my name. . . . I remember once an agent said he needed a trained-animal act. My partner and I brought two dogs, held them under our arms and just roller-skated around with them."

Was he a bad entertainer? Probably not as bad as he makes people believe. On the tenth anniversary of *The Tonight Show* in 1972, he compared career highlights with Johnny Carson and fellow comedians including Jack Benny and Jerry Lewis.

"I think my big highlight is when I played the Jefferson Theater on 14th Street in New York, and I played there for three days and I wasn't closed."

He told Ed Bradley a similar story in 1988 when he was interviewed for *60 Minutes*.

"When I started I had no talent. I worked with a seal.

I worked with a dog. I did a skating act. Yeah, Goldie Fields and Glide. I was Glide. The worst. Anyway I kept changing partners until I was twenty-seven, and then I started playing some good theaters and people discovered that I had a big talent. I was married to her for thirty-eight years."

He talks about some of his early acts in vaudeville.

"It was small-time vaudeville, playing bad theaters and thinking you were good if you played a theater worse than you were. . . . In vaudeville you couldn't say 'damn.' You couldn't say 'hell.' And in those days there were cancellation clauses in your contract. You could get canceled after the first performance. So there was always a sign backstage saying, 'Don't send out your laundry until after the first show.' You never knew if you'd stay.

"I was always canceled. I played in the Follies Theater in Brooklyn. I was doing a single then. I was rehearsing my music at ten o'clock in the morning. The manager heard me and canceled me. *I'm the only act in show business that was canceled before he opened.*"

He went from one wretched act to another. He did buck dancing, hard-shoe dancing, and wood-shoe dancing. He sang and he told jokes. He worked with various animals and on roller skates.

He answered to many names. He was Willy Saks of "Willie Saks and His Little Derby Hat." He was Jackson of "Jackson and Malone," Harris of "Harris and Dunlop." He was first Brown and then Williams of "Brown and Williams"; Jack Harris of "Harris and Kelly," Phil Baxter of "Baxter and Bates," Pedro Lopez of "Pedro Lopez and Conchita."

"If you did seventeen or eighteen minutes, that meant

you had a very good spot on the bill. If you only did twelve minutes, you were number two, which was a bad spot. So when you'd meet an actor on the street—let's say he was playing the Fifth Avenue Theater—you'd say, 'Hey Jim, how you doing at the Fifth Avenue?" He'd say, 'Eighteen minutes.' That meant he had a good spot on the bill."

Finally he met a girl he named Hermosa José (after the cigar). Her real name was Hannah Siegal. They did a ballroom act. She was Jewish, and from an Orthodox family to boot. It led to marriage, which lasted thirty-six weeks or twenty-six weeks depending on when he told the story and to whom he told it. In either case it didn't last very long.

"It wasn't a very good act, and to give you an idea of how little we knew about show business, our opening number was a Russian mazurka. We thought that was a Spanish dance. So we both dressed up in Spanish clothes and did a Russian mazurka. Our second number was an eccentric fox dance. Our third was a cakewalk. We were booked on the small time. We were small-time vaudevillians and we got booked for thirty-six weeks.

"This girl was a very Orthodox Jewish girl. She was seventeen and I was twenty-one. Her father and mother wouldn't let me take her on the road unless I married her. Well, I wasn't going to cancel twenty-six weeks, so I married her. And we played for twenty-six (thirty-six) weeks, but I never slept with her. We slept with a sheet in between us in the room, because it was cheaper than taking two rooms."

That trademark cigar was always ever present.

"The reason I started to smoke is that when I was fourteen, I wasn't doing very well. I was trying to get into show business and I was doing a skating act—a roller-skating act. I used to smoke a cigar, a seven-cent Rocarro, which was a very, very big cigar in those days. It took me all day to smoke that cigar. And it made me look like I was working and doing well. I felt it made me look like an actor.

"I smoke lots of cigars, and I smoke anything that fits into my mouth. I always have a holder. The reason I use a holder is that when I am on the stage or on television, I don't think people like to see the wet end of a cigar. I may not be very funny, but I'm very neat.

"I don't inhale a cigar. A good cigar is well packed. A well-packed cigar goes out three or four times. I smoke on the stage, and if the cigar goes out three or four times onstage, the audience goes out, too. This is a prop as well. When they laugh, I smoke. When they stop laughing, I talk.

The truth is that George never quite knew what to do with his left hand, so he used a cigar. He said as much in an interview for *TV Guide* in 1954. He explains:

"It's many things. A prop. A crutch. A device. A comic's hand must become his straight man. . . . In that time [when I puff on the cigar] the audience heals, digests, interprets, understands, and finally reacts to the joke."

He makes the same point in a 1957 interview with Elias Walker in *The Palo Alto Times.*

"It's a handy device. If I get a laugh with a joke, I just look for the cigar, or twiddle it. If I didn't get a laugh, it's nice to have something to hang on to. When a joke calls for a delayed laugh, I smoke slowly. If that laugh never comes, I swallow. The camera only shows me from the waist up. . . . If it showed the floor I'd lose my reputation. I'm standing up to my ankles in ashes."

In the 1994 winter edition of *Cigar Aficionado* George Burns is interviewed by writer Arthur Marx. Of course, they talked about cigars.

"I smoke a domestic cigar. It's a good cigar. It's called an El Producto. Now the reason I smoke a domestic cigar is because the more expensive Havana cigars are tightly packed. They go out onstage while I am doing my act. The El Producto stays lit. Now if you're onstage and your cigar keeps going out, you have to keep lighting it. If you have to stop your act to keep lighting your cigar, the audience goes out. That's why I smoke El Producto—they stay lit.

"I don't know how much they cost today. I get them for nothing from the Tobacco Institute [in Washington, D.C.]. But about ten years ago they sold for thirty-three cents apiece. Figure inflation in and they're probably fifty cents apiece today."

Arthur Marx asked George the kind of cigar he smoked, when he first started to smoke, and why he started.

"Any five-cent cigar. I was fourteen years old. But I liked a nickel cigar called Hermosa Josés the best. . . . I smoked them because I wanted people to think I was doing well. When they saw me walking down the street smoking a cigar, they'd say, 'Hey, that fourteen-year-old kid must be going places.' Of course it's also a good prop on the stage. That's why so many performers, including your father [Groucho Marx], use them. When you can't think of what you're supposed to do next, you take a puff on your cigar until you do think of the next line.

"[When I started] I'd say two cigars a week would last me. Hermosa Josés were long cigars, and I'd let them go out when I wasn't onstage or trying to impress someone. . . . I've never smoked a cigarette. Just cigars. They're better for you. Today I smoke about ten cigars when I'm not working and about fifteen when I am working."

George's cigar was a Burns signature. So was his self-deprecating and irreverent humor. And so were the obscure cornball songs that he never seemed to finish. He admits to being better able to create comic material than to deliver it.

"I always knew what to do onstage. But I didn't have enough talent to do it myself. I made up a joke, but I couldn't tell it."

Explaining the structure of vaudeville to writer Larry Wilde, he says:

"Well, vaudeville was too grooved for me. The sad part was, if you did a great balancing act, if you were the world's greatest juggler—I think the world's greatest anything should be a star—but you weren't in vaudeville. If you were the world's greatest juggler, you would open the shop or close it. It was wrong. The world's greatest magicians—until Houdini came along—magicians would close the show or open it. Later on they switched the shows around a little bit and the comedy acts used to close the show. Number two act would be a two-man dancing act and the third act was a sketch. The fourth act would be a single woman. The fifth act would be a big act. And then the magician would open intermission, and then the headliner would come on—Sophie Tucker or Blossom Seeley or Norma Bayes."

It all changed in Union City, New Jersey, in 1923 when an unemployed seventeen-year-old Irish-American dramatic actress heard he was looking for a partner for a new comedy act and went backstage to see him. As George Jessel was to say later, "This partnership was made in heaven."

# CHAPTER THREE

# Gracie

*"For forty years my act consisted
of one joke. And then she died.*
—Cited in *The Christian Science Monitor*
(March 12, 1996)

George was surprised by Gracie, bemused by Gracie, but most of all he looked upon himself as her protector. He called her "Googie." She called him Natty. And she became "Googie" to George and to their close friends as well.

"One time she shook me in the middle of the night and said, 'Natty? Would you say something funny? I can't sleep.' At two in the morning my repertoire is a little limited, so I just mumbled 'Googie, googie, googie.' Somehow that made Gracie laugh and somehow that became her name."

She called him "Natty." He called her "Googie." She was born Grace Ethel Cecile Rosalie Allen in San Francisco on the 26th of July, 1906. Her father, Edward Allen, was a song-and-dance man. At thirteen, she was booked for "singles" in the San Francisco area. A year later she joined her three older sisters in an act that later became part of the Larry Riley Company. She specialized in Irish brogue and colleen parts.

She was sixteen years old in 1922 when she was informed by a girlfriend that the act of Burns and Lorraine was breaking up. She was advised by her friend to team up with Lorraine because "Burns is terrible." Gracie, by mistake, walked up to George and said, "I hear you're looking for a new partner."

"I am," George replied. "Why don't you meet me in front of the Palace at twelve tomorrow? We'll have breakfast." When Gracie left she said, "Good-bye, Mr. Lorraine. . . ."

Years later George recounted that first meeting.

"I told her to stop calling me Mr. Lorraine. My name was Burns. And three years later her name was Burns. . . . All my life I was in love with show business. And for the first time I was in love with something else. First of all you've got to have talent. And then you have to marry her. [For Gracie] it was a choice of secretarial school or teaching dancing back home in San Francisco. She didn't have train fare home and hated to type, so my irresistible charm won out. The girl was struck by something in front of an audience. They adored her.

"They loved her. You know there was nothing sexy about Gracie. No big bust or anything. She was just a dainty, nice, Irish girl with blue-black hair, and quick delivery and great, great style.

"I knew entrances. I knew exits. I was able to switch a joke. . . . I was able to think of it, and Gracie was able to do it. That made us a good team. In *The Burns and Allen Show* we didn't have any comedians. They were all actors and actresses. Gracie was a fine actress who played the part of an off-center girl. The character was simply the dizziest dame in the world, but what made her different from all the other dumb Doras was that Gracie played her as if she was totally sane, as if her answers actually made sense. . . . We called it illogic logic."

George and Gracie appeared for the first time together at the Hill Street Theater in Newark, New Jersey, in 1922. Yet her range and scope went far beyond her professional dumbness on radio and screen. She played opposite James Cagney in a serious Irish playlet for a Screen Guild show once, and did very well. Another time the University of Southern California psychology students honored her by voting her Hollywood's most intelligent actress.

Initially George was the comic and Gracie was the "straight" woman. He talked about that first night with Rex Reed in a 1975 interview for the New York *Sunday News.*

"The first night we had forty people out front and they didn't laugh at one of my jokes, but every time Gracie asked me a question they fell out of their seats. So I made her the comic and the act was a hit from that minute on. . . . She was a helluva dramatic actress and sometimes she got tired of being considered a dumbbell. . . . But she went along with the act. Don't forget, she was never dressed up funny like Baby Snooks. She wore beautiful clothes and no matter how zany her lines were, the audience always believed her. That was her power. . . . I used to sit around at 4 A.M. with an army of writers trying to think up a joke and Gracie would walk in and say, 'Isn't that nice?' and everyone would fall on the floor. She was the genius, not me."

In another interview, with Bart Mills of the *Guardian* in 1975, George added some more insight.

"I was never a jerk. I wanted to keep on smoking good cigars, so I gave her the jokes. I couldn't be bad with Gracie on. I knew what to do, but she knew how to do it. There's a whole megillah about being a straight man. It's supposed to be so difficult. Actually, all you've got to have is ears. When the audience stopped laughing, I'd ask Gracie the next question.

"I lie a lot. But when I write about Gracie, I don't have to lie. The truth is believable enough. For forty years it seemed that Gracie and I were always training for our next appearance. Marrying Gracie was the best thing that ever happened to me. I have the feeling she felt the same way—that marrying her was the best thing that ever happened to me.

"I was dressed up *funny*. Told funny *lines*. They laughed at Gracie. So the next show I took off my funny clothes, put on street clothes and gave Gracie the funny lines. And I noticed that if the joke line was sarcastic, sharp, they wouldn't laugh as much, but if it was off-beat, they'd scream.

"A joke like: She says, 'My sister had a baby.' I say, 'Was it a boy or a girl?' And Gracie says, 'I don't know. But I can't wait to get home to find out if I'm an uncle or an aunt!' Stuff like that! They loved it. The audience finds everything, and you can't be a star unles the audience makes you a star."

The Burns and Allen pay envelope for the first three days of their act at the Hill Street Theater was fifteen dollars. In 1940 they were reputed to be making $9,000 a week for their radio act. But if they jelled professionally, George had to keep his emotional feelings on hold. He was not yet technically divorced from Hannah Siegal. And despite turning it into comedy material of sorts—"She was a lovely girl but I wouldn't have married her for a sixteen-week booking"—he never said much publicly except that the marriage didn't work. When a director told George he would have to kiss Gracie, he was miffed.

"I was afraid to kiss her or she'd know how stuck I was on her."

Gracie in turn thought she was in love with Benny Ryan, a talented young Irish dancer. There was another concern as well. To date George had been little more than a failed song-and-dance man. Now he was going to try to be funny. Most of his comic material was borrowed from two joke collections, *Whiz Bang* and *College Humor*. After their uneventful opener, they knocked the audience dead in their second show. George kept his ear to the audience, and Gracie played off his straight lines like a seasoned pro. Gracie Allen had given George Burns the miracle he had been searching for over 25 years. She made him a success at the only thing he ever wanted to be in life.

"Actually I didn't do much work at all. Gracie and I would come out on the stage. I'd ask her, 'How's your brother?' Then I simply stood back and she talked for twenty-two minutes. The audience laughed. When she was through, we both took our bows."

George would soon become a businessman as well as an entertainer. He'd negotiate contracts himself, and would always be on top of all the business dealings of *The Burns and Allen Show*. Replacement acts were now a thing of the past. No longer would he have to keep his bags packed.

"It seemed we were always on a bus or a short-hop train. . . . We dressed in boiler rooms, bathrooms, and closets."

George talked to Ed Bradley about those early days

with Gracie on a segment of *60 Minutes* that first aired on January 6, 1988, then again on January 29, 1996.

"The first day I worked with Gracie, I was a comedian. I wrote the act but they didn't laugh at me. And I changed the act around. The audience found Gracie's character. If Gracie said something sarcastic, they didn't like it. They liked silly things that she said.

"What made us a good combination is my talent was off the stage. I could think of things and Gracie was able to do them. I was a straight man. After the comedian gets through with the joke, I look down at the comedian, then I look at the audience. When I'm really rolling, this was one of my ad-libs:

> BURNS: What beautiful flowers!
> ALLEN: Aren't they lovely? And if it wasn't for you I wouldn't have them.
> BURNS: Me?
> ALLEN: Mm-hmm.
> BURNS: What did I have to do with this?
> ALLEN: Well, it was your idea. You said when I went to visit Clara Bagley to take her flowers. So when she wasn't looking I did.

". . . The audience loved her, and I did, too. I fell in love with the act. I fell in love with Gracie. I fell in love with the audience. I fell in love with show business, and I fell in love with my living."

He first realized that he was totally smitten with Gracie when she told him that she and Benny Ryan were engaged. But Benny was traveling on the road, so George made ample use of his time. He started taking Gracie dancing at night. He could be romantic on the dance floor, yet still proper. He had enormous confidence on the dance floor.

In time it worked. After three years together in what Burns called "vaudeville's big time," he and Gracie were married on January 7, 1926, in Cleveland, Ohio.

"We were in Cleveland. We scheduled it for 8 A.M. But the justice of the peace was steamed because he wanted to go fishing. The guy married us so fast, it was eighty cents on the taxi meter when we pulled up and ninety cents when we left.

"When Gracie and I were in vaudeville, we lived in two-buck-a-day hotels. But for our honeymoon, we'd figure we'd go the classy route—seven dollars a day. We checked into the Slater at 4 A.M., but the clerk said the day didn't start until six. Well, I wasn't going to pay no extra seven bucks. So we sat in the lobby for two hours.

"We never had any problems working together and being married. Gracie never thought I was a good lover, and I wasn't. That was that. . . . Offstage Gracie was never interested in show business. She only cared about it during those minutes she was onstage. I'd worry about makeup, lighting, billing, everything else. When a couple competes—'No, I don't want a pin spot, I want a big spot'—then it's trouble."

Later that year a scout for B. F. Keith Theaters spotted them performing at the Jefferson Theater in New York City, and signed them to a six-year contract with the vaudeville chain.

"You know, lots of people have asked me what Gracie and I did to make our marriage work. It's simple—we didn't do anything. I think the trouble with a lot of people is that they work too hard at staying married. They make a business out of it. When you work too hard at a business you get tired; and when you get tired you get grouchy and start fighting. And when you start fighting, you're out of business.

"Looking back I really don't see why Gracie married me. I was already starting to lose my hair. I had a voice like a frog. I stuttered and stammered. I was a bad small-time vaudeville actor. I guess she must have felt sorry for me.

"Gracie wasn't theatrical offstage. You'd never know she was in show business. She said funny things, but I don't think she ever told a joke. Gracie was an Irish dramatic actress when I met her. She played the part of the kind of dame—a dizzy cluck.

"To Gracie, there were no footlights, no audience. She'd just talk to me. Rather than tell a joke, she'd explain it to you. For example, like the time I came home. I said, 'What are we having for dinner?' She said, 'Roast beef. I just put two roasts in the oven. A big one and a little one.' I said, 'Why?' *Because when the little one burns, that means the big one is done!*'

"Then I'd say to Gracie, 'This family of yours, do they all live together?' She'd say, 'Sure, my nephew, my brothers, and cousins. They all sleep in one bed.' I'd say, 'I'm surprised your grandfather doesn't sleep with them.' 'Oh he did, but he died, so they made him get up.'"

"The secret of her success with an audience was that she always sounded sincere. The things she said seemed to make perfect sense to her. George: 'Did the nurse drop you on your head when you were a baby?' Gracie: 'Oh, we couldn't afford a nurse. My mother had to do it.'"

But there was one problem onstage—George's cigar!

"I had to make sure the smoke from my cigar didn't go in her direction. That's all I really had to worry about because I knew she was good. The biggest thing in my life was meeting Gracie. I don't think I would have made it if I hadn't met her. I would have remained a small-time vaudeville act, and when small-time vaudeville went out, I'd have gone out with it. I might have been a cutter of ladies' garments, but whatever it would have been, it wouldn't be great."

The Burns and Allen stage combination found wide favor with audiences. With the Keith contract intact, they toured the vaudeville circuit both here and in Europe, where they peddled their new act called "Lamb Chops."

"My uncle eats concrete," she once said. "My mother asked him to stay to dinner, but he said he was going to eat up the street."

Another big break occurred in 1929, when they made an unassuming appearance at a party, an appearance that was quite unexpected. It was at the home of Arthur Lyons, and the result would change their lives forever. It was something George would never forget.

"We were [now] getting about four hundred dollars a week. And we were at a party at Arthur Lyons' house, who was handling Jack Benny. We weren't even invited. Jack took us. Arthur Lyons came over and said, 'Fred Allen is supposed to make a short and he can't make it.' He says to Jack, 'If you can go over there tomorrow and do eight minutes, they will give you seventeen hundred dollars.' Jack said, 'I can't go over there tomorrow.' I said, 'We can go!' He said, 'Sure, go ahead!'

"We went there and the set didn't fit our dialogue. It was a living room set, but we were a street corner act, a flirtation act. So we had to improvise. I walked out and Gracie was lifting up plates and ashtrays. I said, 'What are you looking for?' She said, 'The audience.' I said, 'See that lens sticking out of the camera?' She said, 'Yeah.' I said, 'If you look in the lens, that's where the audience is. . . .' She said, 'Oh!' I said, 'Gracie, if we can talk for eight minutes, we can make seventeen hundred dollars.

"I didn't know what to do, and Gracie said, 'Ask me how my brother is.' I said, 'How's your brother?' And she kept talking. She was in the middle of a joke at eight minutes. I looked at my watch and said, 'Hold it! The eight minutes are up.' I looked at the camera and said, 'Ladies and gentlemen, we just made seventeen hundred dollars. Say good night, Gracie!' And Gracie did just that. . . ."

Ed Bradley touched upon a time when George strayed during his forty-year relationship with Gracie and got caught.

"Yeah. OK. I'll tell you. I did. Gracie wanted a centerpiece for the table. I said, 'Silly, we don't need it.' And then I found out from the maid that Gracie knows about this thing I had with this girl. The next day I not only brought home a silver centerpiece for supper. I bought Gracie a diamond ring for $10,000. I gave it to her. She never said a word. She took the diamond ring. She took the centerpiece. And then six or seven years later she said to Mary Benny, 'I wish George would cheat again. I need another centerpiece.' "

Burns and Allen would play themselves in more than a score of films, including fourteen shorts. George Burns had not only survived the doom and gloom of a second-rate vaudeville career, he far survived vaudeville itself—a considerable feat considering that many front rank stars never made it past the vaudeville stage.

At the end of his life this fact continued to give him a healthy perspective.

"Vaudeville didn't put me out of business. See, vaudeville went out of business. The other acts allowed themselves to go out of business. . . . I said the hell with that. I loved what I was doing."

The vaudeville days were now a vanishing ember. Radio days loomed ahead. *The Burns and Allen Show* and show-biz stardom were just a jump start away.

# CHAPTER FOUR

# Burns and Allen

*"I just get good people together and let them do their job.
If I can't help them, I leave them alone."*
— *Variety* (February 7, 1957)

Since they first hit the big time with their now famous "Lamb Chops" act, it was all uphill for George and Gracie. Their five-year contract on the Keith-Orpheum circuit meant they would play to huge crowds all across the country.

George explained the origin of their famous "Lamb Chops" routine:

"The big jokes in those days were *eating* jokes. 'Do you like to love?' 'No.' 'Do you like to kiss?' 'No.' 'What do you like?' 'Lamb chops.' 'A little girl like you, can eat two lamb chops alone?' 'Not alone, but with potatoes I could!' "

"We had a routine about lamb chops, so you would title the act "Lamb Chops." The entire routine went seventeen minutes . . . not wholly about lamb chops . . . it consisted of everything. . . . We used to walk out—I would hold her hand (we were very young in those days—it was a boy-girl act—we weren't married) and she would look offstage and there would be a man there and she would kiss him, and he would kiss her, and he would say good-bye and she would say good-bye, and she would turn around to me and say, 'Who's that?' It got a very big laugh.

"What made it such a good joke is that it set up her character in one line. You knew right away she was a little on the screwy side. We did jokes like that, and finally we got into food and did the little routine about lamb chops. Then we came into New York and opened at the Jefferson Theater and got a five-year contract. That's why 'Lamb Chops' was so important to us—it got us started.

Nineteen twenty-nine was a big year for Burns and Allen. First they made their film debut as a third-choice replacement for first-choice Fred Allen, and for second-choice Jack Benny, in the Vitaphone short *Burns and Allen in Lamb Chops,* excerpted from their vaudeville routine. They were soon the top vaudeville team in the country.

In that same year George and Gracie were invited to perform onstage in England for twenty-one weeks. They also tried out British radio and were a big hit when they performed for the prestigious British Broadcasting Corporation.

Following their successful 1930 stint on British radio, they returned to New York to play the Palace with Eddie Cantor. It was another watershed event for George and Gracie, the result of which placed them flush in the public spotlight.

"We were playing the Palace Theater with Cantor and Georgie Jessel. And Cantor said, 'How would you like to be in the show?' 'Not you. Just Gracie!' I said, 'Sure, providing you do our material. How long do you want

Gracie to do?' He said, 'Five minutes, write it out!' I said, 'I don't have to write it out. You just walk on the show and say to Gracie, 'How is your brother?' and she'll talk for five minutes.' Then the next week we got a job on the Rudy Vallee Show. Then on to Guy Lombardo. And we were in show business."

Their appearances proved so popular that in 1933, CBS offered them their own radio show, which ran for the next seventeen years and consisted of songs and sketches as well as vaudeville routines. The supporting cast included Mel Blanc, Clarence Nash, Richard Crenna, Hans Conried, and Gale Gordon. The live show also went out on the road every so often to broadcast from various cities across the country. Launched on February 15, 1932, *The Burns and Allen Show* remained on the air, usually with a top ten rating for its entire duration.

There were no conflicts of interest. Being husband and wife was the best thing that could have happened to Burns and Allen.

"Some people have to choose between their marriage and career, but our marriage was our career."

And it was. The Burns and Allen stage and radio routine was a reflection of the Burns and Allen personal relationship, only magnified and made into a cartoon.

In 1962 he told Jack Paar on *The Tonight Show* how he was able to make Jack Benny laugh at the drop of a hat.

"On our wedding night, Jack called us from Vancouver. I told him we would like breakfast at ten o'clock up in the room. Scrambled eggs, toast, and marmalade.

'But—' 'And a big pot of coffee.' I hung up. A few minutes later, the phone rings again. 'I know it's late,

Nat, but it's me. Jack. Why did you hang up? I wanted to congratulate you and—' 'And don't forget the orange juice,' I said. And I hung up again. After the third call I let him finish congratulating me. By then he was laughing so hard he almost couldn't get it out. . . . Now if I don't hang up on him he thinks I'm mad at him. [After that] he never stopped laughing. If I said anything he'd fall on the floor. His suits were always at the cleaners."

Burns and Benny had something else in common. They were both Jewish men who had fallen in love with Gentile women. But unlike Jack Benny, who backed away from his true love, Mary Kelly, because of religious reasons, Gracie's Catholicism was not a problem for George. To the contrary, he found no trouble in assuring Gracie that any children they had could be brought up Catholic.

"It didn't make a difference to me. My religion is show business."

The movies also beckoned. In addition to their fourteen shorts, George and Gracie also had cameo or supporting roles in a dozen full-length features.

The first feature was *The Big Broadcast of 1932* for Paramount. Basically, it was a series of vaudeville acts narrated by Bing Crosby. Set in a radio station, it was just an hour long, and was intended to capitalize on radio's booming popularity. Burns and Allen played themselves and did a brief act.

Moreover, the picture marked the first time Gracie appeared as a blonde. The director felt her beautiful black hair was too dark for a black and white film.

The following year they made *International House* with W. C. Fields. In the film there is a scene where George appears without Gracie. It is that hilarious scene

set in a men's clothing store where George is a customer
and W. C. Fields is the clerk:

> BURNS: (entering the shop) I'd like to buy a
> sweater.
>
> FIELDS: A sweater. (He looks around.)
> Sweater? (He picks up a derby and offers it
> to Burns.) Just to give me an idea of the
> size, try this on. (He places it on the head
> of a scowling Burns.)
>
> BURNS: A little too tight.
>
> FIELDS: (Examining the hat and trying it on.)
> That's funny. It fits me perfectly.
>
> BURNS: (icily) I'd like to buy a sweater.
>
> FIELDS: I could give you that (the hat) in
> black. (He picks up a pair of cowboy
> boots.) Here's something in a large size.
>
> BURNS: Listen, I came in here to buy a
> sweater.
>
> FIELDS: (Pushing him into a chair) Sit down.
> Try one on. How does that fit?
>
> BURNS: (trying on the boot) It's a little loose.
>
> FIELDS: You're rather difficult, brother.
>
> Cited in Martin Gottfried, *George Burns and
> The Hundred-Yard Dash.*

George talked about W. C. Fields with Roy Leonard
of WGN Radio.

"Gracie had a little bit she did with W. C. Fields and
another girl in the picture *International House.* The
scene at the table and Gracie hit him with a funny line
in the picture. Leo McCarey was the director at the
time, and they were trying to think of something to say
or do. So I went over to Bill (W. C. Fields) and said,

'Bill, I'll tell you what to do. You got a cup of coffee on the table and a glass of water, a napkin, and a scotch and soda. Why don't you take two pieces of sugar, put it in the water, mix the coffee, drink the scotch and soda, take the napkin, and wipe the other girl's face. From then on, Bill Fields was in love with me."

Then George addressed the question of Fields' unhappiness.

"The unhappiness was largely a delivery. Everybody thought he was. He had this sarcastic way of working. A good story was that when he was young he was a juggler, a comedy juggler. And he went to England. He was in his later twenties, and he was married, and had a very pretty little wife. When he went to England he sort of opened the show. He was a dumb act. He didn't do any talking. At the finish of the act he used to juggle cigar boxes. And his wife fell in love with a comedian. The comedian stole Bill's wife, but Bill stole his delivery. It was the comedian who used to say, 'My little chickadee.' So Bill got the best of that deal."

In addition to *The Big Broadcast of 1932* and *International House,* Burns and Allen were also featured in *Six of a Kind* (Paramount, 1934); *The Big Broadcast of 1936* (Paramount, 1936); *The Big Broadcast of 1937* (Paramount, 1937); *College Swing* (Paramount, 1938): and *Honolulu* (MGM, 1939).

But their most memorable appearance was dancing with Fred Astaire in *Damsel in Distress* (RKO, 1937). Directed by George Stevens and starring Fred Astair and Joan Fontaine, the film won an Oscar for dance director Hermes Pam. George tells Roy Leonard how he was able to impress the great Astaire.

"We were asked to do *Damsel in Distress* with Fred

Astaire, which was very exciting, because Fred is the world's greatest. I basically danced with my right foot. If I used my left foot I would have to go into another business. I got a good right leg and a bad left leg. Like I said, my left leg wanted me to go into another business, and unfortunately my audience agreed with my left leg.

"Anyway there was a dance in vaudeville, the whisk broom. Two guys used to do it onstage and it was great. I figured that if I could get that whisk-broom dance, it would be great in any movie. It was great onstage. I knew it because I watched it; for thirteen weeks I watched that dance, and it was always a riot.

"So I sent for the fellow who had the whisk-broom dance. He came out here and I paid him. I said, 'Will you teach us the whisk-broom dance, and I'll pay you.' He said, 'Sure!' So instead of two people we put Gracie in the middle and the three of us learned this whisk-broom dance.

"Gracie was a great dancer. Gracie was a great Irish dancer, really great. In fact, Gracie's whole family were great Irish dancers. So we got this whisk-broom dance. So before I danced for Fred, I said, 'Fred, I'd like to show you something. I brought a piano player and I brought this dancer, and I brought whisk brooms, and we did this whisk-broom dance. And Fred Astaire loved it. He says, 'That's a great dance.' I said, 'If you want it, you can have it for the movie.' He said, 'Are you kidding? Of course!' So instead of Fred watching my left leg, I taught him how to use the whisk brooms. Then I got the job."

*The Burns and Allen Show* remained one of the top radio shows during its nearly twenty-year run, with 45 million listeners tuning in every week. The live show also went out on the road every so often to broadcast from various cities across the country.

Any old-time radio buff will attest that some of their routines rank among the true classics. In the May 1963 issue of *McCall's,* George reiterates the evolution of Gracie's role to writer Cleveland Amory.

"In the beginning Gracie was the straight, and I had the lines. But I saw they weren't laughing at my answers but at Gracie's questions. I began to wonder what would happen if she had the jokes, so we reversed it. Actually, Gracie never played a dumb girl. She was always sincere, with her own kind of illogical logic. Her dialogue may not have made sense to anybody else, but it made sense to her, and she thought everybody was off center but her.

George explains the difference between being a comedienne and being an actress who can do comedy.

"A big difference. Take Lynn Fontaine. She's a great actress, but she also played a dumb dame in *Dulcy* and made you believe her. When Gracie played . . . Gracie wasn't dumb . . . in fact, Gracie thought she was terribly smart. Gracie was different. Gracie thought everybody was out of step but her. She was always helping people. She was always sorry for you. Like if she would say, 'My sister got up in the middle of the night, she screamed, she looked down at her feet, and they turned black.'

"You would say to her, 'What did she do?' She was sorry for you for asking the question. She thought you were pretty dumb not to know what to do if your feet turned black. 'She took her stockings off and went to sleep again.' When Gracie would take pepper and put it in the salt shaker and salt in the pepper shaker, she would look at you like you had two heads. Her reasoning was people always get mixed up, and now when they do they are right. She knew what she was doing. . . . We call that illogical logic. It made sense, but it only made sense to Gracie."

He tells writer Larry Wilde how Gracie's character evolved.

". . . When we first went together, half of the jokes didn't fit her at all. It took a good year to get her into character. That doesn't mean it took a year to do a good act, but it took a year to get the wrong words out of Gracie's mouth. Even though you knew some of the jokes were wrong, you couldn't take them out because your act wouldn't be long enough. You would have to leave in some of the wrong jokes until you found the right ones.

". . . You couldn't underline a word for Gracie. She never read anything the same way twice. Jack Benny once came down—we were playing Newark. She said some joke and he says to Gracie, 'This is the third time; I always come down for that joke.' "

One of their running gags during the early 1930s, had Gracie going from show to show looking for her lost brother. One week it might be *The Eddie Cantor Show,* the following week it could be *The Jack Benny Program.* Another time it might be Yankee Stadium. There was no telling where she might appear in pursuit of her brother. She was so successful that her real brother, an accountant in San Francisco, was so besieged by the press that he eventually had to go into hiding.

In 1938 she ran for Governess of the State of Coma.

In 1940 she entered the presidential race, and 100,000 turned out for her convention in Omaha. When asked what party she was with, she answered, "Same old party—George Burns."

# CHAPTER FIVE

# Jack Benny

*"Even though Jack was one of the biggest stars in show business for most of his life, and rubbed elbows with presidents and royalty, it was the little things in life that were important to him."*
—Burns, in his introduction to
*Jack Benny: An Intimate Biography* by Irving Fein (1975)

Besides Gracie, George loved to talk about his bosom buddy Jack Benny. No interview was complete without bringing up the man he considered to the best comedian around.

Born Benny Kubelsky in Waukegan, Illinois, he broke into show business as a serious musician. Unlike his other vaudeville contemporaries he had a middle-class childhood and grew up in a happy home. He received his show business stripes during World War I, when he performed in a review for the Great Lakes Naval Station doing a comedy sketch. The Great Lakes Review was a big hit.

At the end of the war he returned to vaudeville as a monologuist. He called his act "Ben. K. Benny, Fiddletology and Fun." When a top vaudeville star named Ben Benny complained to the Vaudeville Managers

Protective Association, Benny Kubelsky became Jack Benny.

There was a marked contrast between the two friends. While Benny was funny on the stage, but very serious offstage, George was serious onstage—he handled the entire mechanics of his shows, both business and professional—but was enormously funny offstage. He could make Jack crack up at will.

Over the years, George Burns told many Jack Benny anecdotes to interviewers. The following is just a small sampling:

On explaining the longevity of their friendship:

"There's a reason we've been such close friends for fifty-five years. We never see each other."

On doing radio and TV specials: "Jack had a show on radio and television for more consecutive years than anyone else in history. When he no longer wanted to do a weekly show, he did specials. But he never called them that. To me, he said, 'A special is when they knock down the price of lettuce from ninety-nine cents to seventy-nine cents.' "

On his way with women: "In the early days Jack played the Orpheum circuit and slept with every girl from coast to coast."

On telling Jack Benny a joke: "If you told Jack Benny a joke, he wouldn't laugh. But if you told Jack Benny at the spur of the moment that something happened, that would make him laugh. Like when he came in the club. I said, 'Hello, Jack!' He said, 'I didn't sleep last night.' I said, 'How did you sleep the night before?' He said, 'The night before I slept great!' I said, 'Sleep every other night!' That would get him.

"I went to Jack Benny's house. There were about two

hundred people at a party. And Jack calls me aside and says, 'George, the party isn't moving!' I say, 'The party's moving fine. Everybody is drinking. Everybody's talking.' And he got very angry. He said, 'Look! I'm in show business, too. I know if a party moves. This party isn't moving! To have a little fun, I'd thought I'd say, 'Why don't you go upstairs, take off your pants and come down in your shorts, with Mary's hat on, and play the violin.' He said, 'Do you think that will make it move?' I said, 'Of course!'

"So I told everybody, 'Jack is coming down in his shorts, with Mary's hat on, playing the violin. Don't pay attention to him.' Down came Jack with the violin, nobody looked at him. He fell on the floor and started to laugh and said, 'George, now the party is moving!' "

"He was my closest friend. Jack's sense of humor was one of the things that made him. We're sitting and talking once and he starts to laugh. I said, 'What are you laughing at? I'm not saying anything yet.' He says, 'But you're not saying it on purpose.' He was quite a riot, Jack Benny!"

On transition from radio to TV: "Jack was a very strong personality on the stage. He didn't look it. He was a powerhouse. When the [Ronald Colmans] lived next door, this is on radio, you heard a sound effect. One, two, three, four, coming down eight steps. Or when he went over to borrow a cup of sugar, he had a tin can. He is walking on the pavement. Then you heard somebody drop a dime in the tin cup and Jack says, 'Thank you!,' and keeps walking to the Colmans' house. Nobody else could do that on radio. You would lose your audience with a pause like that."

"Jack Benny should get the credit for making sound effects an important part of the story. Before Jack started using sound effects everything would have to be explained in the dialogue. . . . But Jack started using sound effects for effect. . . . Once, I remember, Jack was on our show and he was supposed to be proposing marriage to Gracie. 'I'd better get down on my knees and propose to you before George gets here,' he said. Then listeners heard the creaking sound of an old, rusty door being opened. 'Darn it,' he continued, 'I'm too late, I heard a door open.'

" 'Oh no, Jack,' Gracie told him, 'that was your knees.' "

On being nervous: "I never get nervous. You get nervous, you've got to have talent. Gracie got nervous! Jack Benny got nervous. I've got talent. You ask me questions, I'm able to answer them. When you worked with Gracie or Jack, you had to learn to time your jokes. I've got talent. But I haven't got that kind of talent."

On charity: "Jack Benny was always doing something for charity. He would appear at lottery drawings—in New Jersey he once gave away a million dollars, then fainted. Isaac Stern said that when Jack Benny was onstage in tails in front of ninety great musicians, he looks like the world's greatest violinist. It's a shame he has to play."

George made quite a name for himself in movies late in his career, capturing an Oscar for *The Sunshine Boys* in a role that ironically was written for his friend Jack Benny. But Jack did well in the movies. In 1939 he played the title role in *Charlie's Aunt*. It meant dressing in a woman's clothes.

Gotch-ya-Gracie!
Some comedic fun—
According to George, Gracie
was far more than
a comedienne;
she was a great actress.

Dapper George
and
stylish Gracie—
"How far to Altoona?"

Burns & Allen. "Professionals at work"

*The Burns and Allen Show* made a successful jump from
radio to television in 1950. (George, Gracie and an unidentified actor)

Just a Love Nest—
Cozy & Warm.
Their famous radio & T.V.
theme song was written by
Otto Harbach and Louis A. Hirsh
for the 1920 musical comedy *Mary*
(only the music was played
on the show).

Burns & Allen
publicity shot.

George and Gracie
appear with
their good friend
Jack Benny in
*College Holiday,*
one of the many films
they did for Paramount
in the 1930's.

Gracie asks George for some help with her homework—
scene from *College Holiday.*

Gracie talks
to George about
her relatives.

*Sgt. Pepper's Lonely Hearts Club Band*
(1978). George appeared with Peter
Frampton, The Bee Gees and other
rock stars. He mused, "Peter Frampton
paid his manager that year more than
Al Jolson made in his lifetime. When
you make $52 million you can go
into show business for one year, buy
yourself a country and become king."

On February 15, 1932,
George and Gracie gave
their first performance on
their own radio show.
During nearly twenty years
on radio, they attracted an
estimated audience of more than
45 million listeners.

Young and in love.
After appearing together for
three years in vaudeville, George and
Gracie were married in Cleveland
in 1926. She called him "Nattie;"
he called her "Googie."

George and his trusty cigar
(circa 1940).
When he was ninety-eight
he was still smoking about
ten cigars a day—
fifteen when he was working.

"I like young people—I don't think it's good when older people just hang around each other comparing gravy stains."

*The Sunshine Boys* (1975).

The nightclub natural: George at the zenith of his nightclub years. At his stand-up debut at Harrah's, Lake Tahoe, he quipped, "Ladies and gentlemen: This is the first time I ever played a nightclub, and I hate people who come out and say they're nervous. . . but I am."

*The Sunshine Boys:* 1975 (A Best Supporting Actor Oscar for George). Burns said, "I'm perfect for the part. They're looking for an old Jewish vaudevillian, and I'm an old vaudevillian. . . The character of Al Lewis fits me like a glove."

*Oh, God! Book II:* 1980.
George, as God, returns to enter the troubled life of a little girl, assigning her the task of coming up with a slogan that will revive interest in him. The slogan? "Think God."

Publicity shot,
circa 1983.

The sprightly old rogue:
"People ask me why I don't go out with women my own age,
and I tell them the truth. There are no women my age."

"He really enjoyed making that picture; sometimes after spending all day on the set, he'd stop at my house on the way home to have a drink. The hardest thing about making that movie, he told me, was going to the bathroom. With all the petticoats and underwear and the girdle he had to wear, it took him half an hour to undress and another hour to go to the men's room or the ladies' room."

His one classic picture was *To Be or Not to Be* with Carole Lombard and Robert Stack. Because Jack Benny never really considered himself to be an actor, he had to be talked into doing the film by the director, Ernst Lubitsch, who told Benny he wrote the part just for him.

"Jack was so nervous that after two days he'd run out of fingernails to bite. Just before one take he turned to Robert Stack and asked his advice on how to play a certain scene. 'I'd like to help you, Mr. Benny,' Stack told him, 'but this is only my second movie. . . .' He was so good in the film that when his father saw his son playing a Nazi officer, he got up and walked out of the theater."

So much of what Burns said about his friends lends itself to comedic monologue. But he is totally poignant when he recalled Jack Benny's death while talking with Larry King.

"It was sudden for me. I was there the night he died. Mary came down and said, 'Jack just died.' I said, 'I'm going up to see him.' She says, 'You can't go up. The doctor says nobody can go up.' I says, 'Mary, I've known Jack Benny longer than the doctor.'

"I went upstairs to Jack's room. There was Jack

Benny with his hands like this (indicating folded hands in front of him), and his head on the side. It was like he just told a joke and was timing a laugh. And he was gone."

Eight months after he had open-heart surgery, he was interviewed by Barbara Walters on *The Today Show*. Walters talked lovingly about Jack Benny, which brought tears to George's eyes. Mentioning George's recent surgery, she said how happy she was to be able to thank him while he was "still among us."

George nodded and rasped out thanks in return, although he clearly didn't like it. After Walters' interview, writer Dotson Rader mentioned that he thought Walters had been insensitive, talking to Burns as if he had one foot in the grave. Accordingly, George began talking.

"Yeah, Jack was a very kind, gentle, warm man. That's what made Jack . . . the papers around the world made such a fuss about it [Benny's death]. He got such *newspaper* space. . . . Never anything like it. Everybody went crazy. Australia, and . . . and it wasn't because he was the *greatest* comedian in the world that died. Jack's gentleness was the thing that caught on. Jack Benny does things I think of, but wouldn't do."

What he said next was revealing: "He's a nicer man than me, than anybody. Jack would sit in his hotel room when he was on the road, and it would mean *nothing* for Jack to write fifty or sixty or seventy postcards to people. One of the girls told me this. Jack and I have the same doctor. Every once in a while Jack drops in there with a cake under his arm and sits around, and the nurses make coffee, and they talk. I'd like to say that, but I never think of it. And if I'd think of it I'd say, yeah, they don't want coffee and cake! But he *does* it. He did all kinds of things like that. Jack went so fast. So fast. Who was to know?"

When Rader pressed further about Walters' comment, Burns ignored his objection. But Walters had "rankled him." Then George replied:

"I knew her father. I don't think that she knew that I knew him." He winked at Rader slyly. "Yeah, I knew him as a cardplayer at the club. What could I say, 'Your old man had a terrific hand at poker? I *gambled* with him?' I don't even know what he *did* for a living. Maybe he just played cards."

While he adored Jack Benny, his relationship with Jack Benny's wife, Mary Livingstone (Sadie Marks), was not nearly as cordial. Neither cared for one another but for public consumption it behooved both to be polite to each other. Only after both Jack and Mary were gone did he give an inkling of his true feelings toward her:

"I don't think Mary was ever really a happy person. . . . I often wondered if Jack knew Mary had very little talent."

Finally he sums up his love for Jack Benny in his introduction to Irving Fein's book *Jack Benny: An Intimate Biography.*

"We knew each other for about fifty-five years, and he was the warmest, the most gentle human being I ever met in my life. I really feel fortunate to have had him as a friend for that many years. Jack and I laughed together, we played together, we worked together, we ate together, and in the entire fifty-five years I never walked out on Jack when he played the violin, and he never walked out on me when I sang a song. Now that's really putting friendship to the test.

"Jack Benny was a beautiful man to the whole world, but to me he was something special. It's hard for me to believe that he's gone, but it will never be the same without him."

# CHAPTER SIX

# On Writers and Comedians

*"I could clear this situation up in a minute,*
*but my writers would kill me."*
—Cited in *Say Goodnight, Gracie* by
Cheryl Blythe (1986)

In addition to being a performer, George Burns was also a first-rate writer of comedy. As such he always had a healthy respect for writers. He related the following anecdote to Dalton Rader, then a young writer himself in the mid-1970s en route to an NBC interview.

"I like writers, it's a hard business to break into. . . . There was a guy named Jerry Wald. . . . Jerry Wald wanted to write a newspaper column, see. So he went to Walter Winchell, who was very big then. And Jerry says, 'Say, Mr. Winchell, how do you get famous in this business? I mean, how do you do it?' And Winchell liked him. And he says, 'Kid, you go after the biggest son of a bitch you know. You *kill* him!' So Jerry Wald did his first column. And it was a terrible attack on Walter Winchell! Ha ha. True story. Now Rex [Reed] is going after Frank [Sinatra]. Same thing. I like Rex. He wears nice clothes. . . ."

He explained the difference between being a straight man and a monologuist to writer Larry Wilde in *The Great Comedians Talk About Comedy*. For George, good writing and good comedy were no laughing matters.

"Well, anybody can be a straight man if he hears well. You just have to wait for the laughs. A straight man just repeats the questions and the comedian gets the laughs, and you just wait for them and don't let them die completely at the tail end of the laugh.

"The difference is that the monologuist has no help—you have to get up there on your own two feet and tell your jokes."

Burns also explained how he supervised his writers, and why his writers were of such high quality.

"I knew exactly which way we were going and I steered the writers in that direction. They would write it here—three or four writers—at the typewriter. When writers take work home . . . let's say you have a scene you want to write. They bring in the scene, and you've got four writers and you have to rewrite the scene. Sometimes there is a little resentment because you are taking out a joke that is his favorite—that I don't think is in character or something. You've got discontent. When you sit down from scratch with four writers, nobody knows who said this or that. I found out that's the best way for me . . . for what I'm doing.

"You paid more money to writers so that you got better material. For instance, we had a sad moment once in radio—our rating dropped. We were getting, at that time, around fifteen or sixteen thousand dollars for the package. That was the first time, the only time, in our career that we couldn't get a job, and the ratings dropped.

"Finally, the Morris Office, Bill Murray, said he had a job for us six months later for Swan Soap on radio for seventy-five hundred dollars. Well, I took the job. I paid Paul Whiteman and his band twenty-five hundred dollars a week. Tony Martin was just starting out and I paid him a couple of hundred a week, and I think Bill Goodwin was our announcer.

"I paid my writers four thousand per week and got the best I could get. I lost money that season, but our rating started climbing again, and the next season we got ten thousand per week. I finally got back into the money again. I found out why our rating dropped. What happened was that our jokes were too young for us. You see Gracie and I had two children then, but we were still doing a street corner act . . . and you can't do that. You've got to be your age in show business. You can't be any younger than you are supposed to be, nor any older.

"We told a lot of jokes that were all right for a young boy and girl, but not good for a married woman. Like Bill Goodwin coming out and making love to Gracie . . . well, the audience knew we were married and they wouldn't accept it. For instance, Gracie once said to me when she was thirty-five, 'I can't continue to play this character.' I asked her why and she said, 'Because I'm not thirty-five. I said, 'Gracie, if you were silly or offbeat when you were eighteen, what makes you think you would be any smarter when you are thirty-five?'

"The only difference is when you are eighteen, you can have a little whistle on and a fellow goes to kiss you and you say, 'I'll blow that and the cop will come! You blow it and say, 'Well, it's broken from last night.' When you're thirty-five you tell jokes about cooking, about roast beef in the oven. . . . When we went on for Swan Soap, we were married. We had two children, Ronnie and Sandy . . . and it was an entirely different thing altogether, and your writing is entirely different."

A consummate comedic strategist himself, Burns had some definite opinions on his fellow entertainers.

"I like comedians that don't sweat. I like guys who take it easy, who look like they're not getting paid. For instance, a guy like Don Rickles. He sweats. But he's got to work that way. And he moves. He talks fast. I don't sweat. I just stand there, very, very easy. And when I walk out the people all stand up. They give me a standing ovation. They say, *"Look, he walks, too.*

"Shecky Greene does it easy. I don't even know him very well, but I go out to see him. I think Buddy Hackett is a very funny guy. Joey Bishop is funny."

"I'm a big believer in honesty. The biggest mistake you can make if you are eighteen or nineteen . . . you can take Jack Benny's delivery but don't take his words, because his words are for a seventy-year-old man. First you have something yourself. You gotta take . . . a little bit of Bob Hope—the way he looks at an audience after telling a joke—or Durante's turns, or Jack Benny folding his arms, or whatever you want to take, but only if you can do it—so it fits you—it gives you something new—the combination. But don't finish the way they do. Have your own way.

Burns also felt that what a comedian says and what he does are not as important as *how* he *says* it and *how* he does it.

"[The audience can sense it.] Of course, when you walk out and you are important, they know you are important. It's just like Jack Benny. . . . Jack can walk out on the stage and not tell a joke but say, 'I went in today and I got a piece of roast beef, and it was delicious.' If he stops after the word 'delicious,' and pauses long enough, they'll laugh. The audience will be afraid that they have missed a joke.

". . . the funny thing is, if you are not defeated the audience finally digs it. They may not laugh at your first couple of jokes, but you finally get to them. . . . You don't start out to be a hit—there's no such thing as that. You don't get up in the morning on the fifth of January at ten after two and say, 'I'm going to be a star!' . . . You must love what you are doing. If you work hard enough, you must get better.

"Of course I was very fortunate that I met Gracie when I was about twenty-seven. I was a small-time actor until then and had no idea of getting as far as I did in show business . . . never planned. *You* have nothing to do with it—it's the audience. As I said before, the audience made me find a character for Gracie, and it's the audience that makes you a star even if you do not want to be one. They're the ones that do it.

"I can do anything to Jack Benny and make him laugh, and there are a lot of people who can do anything to me and make me laugh. I've gone to all these night clubs and watched different fellas work. Shecky Greene—it's impossible not to laugh at Shecky Greene. He's so funny . . . and he's clever. He can say anything. He can dance and he can sing and he's wild and he can take falls, but he's basically funny. You see there are comedians who are very good but they are not funny . . . to me. There are guys, I look at them and say, 'Great mechanic.' He knows his exits and entrances, and knows music and how to build it up and bring it down, knows how to quiet an audience, knows all the tricks, but he's not funny."

Larry Wilde asked George Burns if intelligence had anything to do with being a successful comedian.

"I think so. You don't have to analyze your delivery but you have to analyze your attitude? You say to yourself, 'What's funny about this joke?' I don't mean the wording, but what's the attitude? You say to yourself, 'What's my *feeling*?' If you can't analyze, then you're just reciting—just *telling* a joke. I hate a pointed joke . . . that's right on the nose.

"For instance, the funniest routine I have ever done was at a dinner for George Jessel. I got up and said, 'I didn't know there was going to be a mixed audience. Now that there are ladies out there, I'm sure there must be a clean anecdote that I can tell about Jessel.' And I kept talking, and I couldn't find anything clean to say about him, and I didn't say anything dirty either. But the audience knew I had a problem. The audience made it dirty.

"I said, 'When Jessel played Vancouver with Blaskey's Redheads, there was this dame in the act—she was a contortionist—and it gets very cold in Vancouver. From there he went to Portland.' It was that kind of thing, and it is a good example of what [was] said. And you have to have intelligence to work that out."

In an interview with Larry Wilde, he reversed an earlier statement when he complained that "comedians have no place to be lousy anymore."

"I've changed my mind about that. It's a very good thing there aren't a lot of places to be lousy anymore, because if there are places to be lousy, you *stay* lousy. Comedians have to be good, *fast* today. And the kids make it, and they don't have to play all the little towns. In the old days, there was no such thing like Bobby Darin coming into show business, a kid of twenty-two, and being a star . . . or Ann-Margret. It happened in pictures—Mary Pickford. You went through it step by step. It took seven or eight years. Nobody made it overnight.

George had little patience with comedians who used dirty language or employed foul mouth routines. "[Audiences] can laugh at the joke and not like you as a human being. You tell a dirty joke and the people laugh, but they resent it. It's the wrong kind of laughs, and the wrong kind of laughs will kill you. Let's say in a night club where you are doing some bit too risqué—you are shocking an audience into a laugh, a disappointed laugh.

"I don't want to mention any names but there is one comedian who is real dirty. I went to see him, and the audience screamed at him. But I don't think they liked him. You don't love him. There's no affection. You see Benny, you like Benny. There's something warm about Benny. Jimmy Durante—you want to take him home with you. Bob Hope. But then there are other guys who are great comedians who are funny, and they don't have to be dirty but they are."

George was fond of a writer named John P. Medbury, whose work he admittedly used from time to time. Once, however, it almost backfired on him.

"Years ago there was a columnist for the Hearst papers named John P. Medbury. He wrote two or three columns, one of which was called 'He and She.' Here's the joke:

> HE: A funny thing happened to my mother in Cleveland.
>
> SHE: I thought you were born in Buffalo.

Good joke. We used it in our act for a while, and Jesse Block is using it at the same time. He calls me up one day and says, 'That's our joke. You've got to stop using it.' I say, 'What do you mean? It was in John Medbury's column. We both stole it from the same place.' And Jesse says, 'Yeah, but I stole it from the first edition.' "

He frowned on ethnic humor, unless it was Jewish humor like the one he told Dotson Rader in an *Esquire* magazine interview.

"I'll tell you a story. There was this little old Jew that fell in a barrel of shit. And he yells, 'Fire! Fire!,' see? And when they pull him out of the barrel, they say, 'Why did you holler fire? There wasn't any fire.' And the old Jew says, 'Would anyone have saved me if I hollered 'shit'?'"

Some final words about comedy: "If something makes you laugh, I think you will laugh as loudly as you did forty years ago. I don't think there is any difference between the volume of laughter."

"I always had a natural sense of humor—even when I worked with the Pee Wee Quartet when we were kids. I was able to get laughs on the street corner, but not on the stage. I was self-conscious about being onstage. If I was invited to somebody's house—to a party—I was very good. Prepared stuff was hard for me to do. A lot of people are very funny if they don't have to stick to the words—if they have to stick to the words it's another ball game."

George believed that people with a vested interest in

your being funny—namely the price of a ticket—were easier to please than those who didn't. "It's easier to make an audience laugh that pays to come in, because they are paying to see you. They get dressed, and they put on a collar and tie, and they get in their cars and pay so much to see you—they like your act. It's very tough to make an audience laugh that doesn't pay, because they are very critical."

# CHAPTER SEVEN

# The Vaudeville Gang

*"If I'd have taken my doctor's advice and quit smoking*
*when he advised me to, I wouldn't have lived*
*to go to his funeral."*
—Cited in *Cigar Aficionado* (Winter 1994)

George Burns was a fortunate man by any standard.
He had a devoted wife, two loving children whom
George and Gracie adopted, and lively and interesting
friends. He knew and worked with the greatest entertainers of the twentieth century. Talented and polished
showmen who enriched not just his life, but the lives of
millions and millions of people the world over. Entertainers one and all, they spanned the time of more than
half a century: names like George Jessel, Jack Benny,
Eddie Cantor, Sophie Tucker, Bob Hope, Milton Berle,
Fanny Brice, Danny Thomas, Frank Fay, Jimmy Durante, the Marx Brothers, Danny Kaye, Judy Garland,
Carol Channing, Walter Matthau. The list goes on and
on.

His regular table in the dining room of the Hillcrest
Country Club in Los Angeles was a mecca for show
business types, where comedians like Jack Benny,
George Jessel, Eddie Cantor, and Al Jolson held court.

"I've been a member of the Hillcrest Country Club about fifty-five years. I used to sit at the same table as Jolson and Eddie Cantor. I go there every day. Play a little bridge. Then I go home around three o'clock. Take off my hair. Put it on the block. I go to bed, get up at five-thirty, and have a double martini. Then when I go out I have a double martini."

Burns considered Al Jolson the greatest entertainer he ever saw. He discloses some of the reasons why to Larry King.

"Al Jolson came from a Jewish family. His father was a cantor. He blackened up and sang, "I Got a Mammy in Alabamee" and made people cry. That's how great he was. He convinced the audience that he had a Mammy in Alabamee.

"Gracie and I are playing in Denver. And we are on number three. We were a little man-and-woman act. We were playing the big time, but we're a small act. Al Jolson is playing at another theater. We got two tickets and we ran over to see Jolson. We never took off our makeup. We got there about . . . ten minutes after nine. Nine-thirty, no Jolson! A quarter to ten, the people are applauding. Finally Jolson walks on the stage full of snow. It was snowing in Denver. He told the audience he went to a party and got carried away. He was talking, and he's sorry he was late.

"He said, 'Do you mind if I put on my makeup here?' He stripped to the waist up. Put on blackface. Did about twenty minutes of the show and then said, 'Wait a minute! You know what happens. The horse wins the race. The fellow gets the girl. Do you want to see that, or do you want me to entertain you?' They all said, 'Entertain us!' He brought the Golden Girls out on the stage. He said, 'You girls who have dates, go about your business.' Three or four girls left. He said, 'The rest of you sit down on the floor.'

"He entertained the audience until one o'clock in the morning. At one o'clock in the morning he says, 'I'm going to take off my makeup and I'm going next door in the restaurant. There is a piano in there. I'll bring out the piano player and sing a few songs, too.' Everybody ran out after him. *There was nobody like him.*

"Jolson was a tough guy, though not a bad guy to me. He always had the water running in the dressing room. He never wanted to hear another act being a hit. That's true. So he never heard applause, or anything before or after. Then he walked on the stage.

"I used to see him in the club. I said, 'Jolie! I've seen everybody. You're the greatest entertainer I've ever seen in my life.' And I complimented him. And he says to me, 'George,' he says, 'you know they don't allow sturgeon in California! Do you like sturgeon?' I said, 'I love sturgeon!' He said, 'I sent for two hundred dollars' worth of sturgeon from Barney Greengrass. Do you want some sturgeon for lunch?' I say, 'Sure!' Well, I had sturgeon about two or three times a week. I kept complimenting Jolson. It got so that I liked sturgeon better than I liked Jolson.

"Then Jolson did the sound track for *The Jolson Story,* and I told him that it was the greatest thing I ever saw in my life. He stopped and said, 'You can buy your own sturgeon now, kid. I'm a hit again.'

"You had to see Jolson. He wasn't the greatest talent in the world. He could only do two things. He was a great comedian, a great light comedian. But nobody appreciated that because his singing was so great, and you forgot all those laughs.

"When he did blackface, everybody else did blackface. Cantor did blackface when he did blackface. Cantor went through the Ziegfeld roof after seeing Jolson. He blackened up and did his face."

Eddie Cantor and his wife, Ida, lived within two blocks of George and Gracie.

"Cantor had a lot of vitality. But Cantor wasn't in Jolson's class. Cantor was managed by Max Hayes. When Cantor went to Ziegfeld's, it was a great hit. Max Hayes blackened up everybody. He had a hit radio show, *The Chase and Sanborn Show.*

"[In vaudeville] Cantor had a cute opening bit. He'd come onstage with a deck of cards and ask for volunteers from the audience. He'd give cards to four or five people and tell them to stand up and hold them over their heads, but warn them not to let them see what they were. And then while they were standing there holding these cards over their heads, he'd ignore them completely. He'd start singing. 'Oh, How She Could Yacki Hicki Wicki Wacki Woo.' It wasn't exactly a love song. It took the audience to realize that the card trick was no card trick, just people standing up holding cards over their heads."

George admired Sophie Tucker. Like himself, she wouldn't do anything that wasn't her age. "I allow myself to get old. It's very important," George would always say.

"Her voice was so strong she could audition for a part in New Jersey without leaving New York. . . . Sophie Tucker used to sing, 'Papa Goes Where Mama Goes or Papa Doesn't Go Out Tonight,' when she was twenty.

But she had nice things, very sexy, and sex kept him home. When she was forty-five she still sang the same song, but she had a gun in her hand. The gun kept him home.

"Now Blossom Seeley didn't allow herself to grow old. Blossom Seeley was a tremendous talent. She got down to sing on one knee long before Jolson. In fact, in one show when Jolson was there, she got down on one knee to sing, and Jolson sang with her. And she got up and he didn't. Blossom Seeley was booked on *The Ed Sullivan Show*. She was eighty-two years old and she sang the same song, 'Toddling the Toddle-O.' You can't 'Toddle the Toddle-O' when you're eighty-two. You can 'toddle' until you're about twenty-one, and then you walk very slowly."

On Jimmy Durante: "His nose was so big he was afraid people would laugh at him. And they did. It made him rich. Or how about mistaking the imprint of Jimmy's nose in the Sidewalk of the Stars for a pothole?

"They loved him. A religious man, nicely married. No scandal about him. And everybody loved him. He sang great. I saw him before they were Clayton, Jackson, and Durante. He had a little band. He used to play in a rathskeller on 121st. Clayton, Jackson, and Durante got together.

"Clayton, Jackson, and Durante were playing in some café in New York and were getting seven thousand dollars a week, but they didn't do business for two weeks. So when they went for their pay—and the gangsters owned this café—they gave Clayton $10,000 instead of $14,000. Clayton said they wanted the whole amount, so the guy picked up the money and hit Clayton in the face. Clayton picked up the money and hit him back in the face again. Said he wanted $14,000. So this little murderer not only gave Clayton $14,000 he gave him a Cadillac car. The moral is, always hit a gangster in the face with $10,000."

While Burns admired Frank Fay, he was not above playing a typically pointed prank at Fay's expense: According to George, "Fay was great, but he was a mean son of a bitch."

"Frank Fay was a great, great comedian. But he was a tough guy. When he got divorced from Barbara Stanwyck, he got on the stand and they said, 'What do you do for a living?' He said, 'I'm the world's greatest comedian.' So somebody at the club said, 'Frank! Did you say you were the world's greatest comedian?' He said, 'I had to! I was under oath.'

"And Frank Fay didn't like Jews and he didn't like blacks. But he was very religious. I used to sit in The Brown Derby, and just before his food came I mentioned something about eight or nine people who are dead. And every time you'd mention somebody, he'd bless himself and say a little prayer. When his food got cold, I'd leave."

In their heyday, Burns ate lunch every day at the corner table in the Men's Grill at Hillcrest. The only Hillcrest members allowed to eat there were comedians. In a recent article in *Cigar* magazine, Burns told Arthur Marx, Groucho's son, who he thought was the funniest of the bunch.

"To me the funniest man at the table was [George] Jessel. I have to say this because your father thought he was the funniest, but Jessel was funnier. He had a strange delivery, and he didn't tell jokes per se. But he had a delivery that nobody else could emulate. For example, I was sitting at the table one day—I'm going back a lot of years—and it was only nine o'clock in the morning. Jessel was at the bar. He was having his third brandy. I said to him, 'Jesus, George, nine o'clock in the morning and you're already on your third brandy. What is this?' And he said, 'Didn't you hear? Norma Talmadge died.' (Norma Talmadge was his former wife.) 'That was 35 years ago,' I reminded him. And he replied, 'I still miss her.'

"He was a strange fellow. . . . He took a shot at a doctor once—the one who Norma ran away with. And he missed the doctor and hit the gardener two blocks away. The gardener took Jessel to court. And the judge asked him, 'Mr. Jessel, how can you aim at a doctor and hit a gardener two blocks away?' And Jessel replied, 'Your Honor, I'm an actor, not Buffalo Bill.' "

"Mr. Television," Milton Berle:

"Milton Berle would host a fundraiser to prevent chapped lips. . . . Many performers wouldn't do his show because Milton did everything to remain the center of attention except shoot the guest star. Someone once wrote that the man who once wrote that nothing was impossible never tried to get between Milton and the camera. Mahalia Jackson was a wonderful gospel singer; she sang about trouble and hardship and having faith in the Lord. But until she worked with Milton she wasn't aware he was a genius, but if she were ever on his show again, she said, 'He'd better not genius all over me.'

"He came to TV when it was brand new. There was nobody in television at the time. He could thank his mother for being there. Well, his mother used to sit in the audience and stand up. His mother was a very attractive lady. She's sitting in the audience next to some man, and the guy is making a play for her—playing with her knee. She didn't pay any attention to him because Milton was on. And she applauded, she stood up, and she laughed at the right spot. When she got through, she slapped the man in the face. But not when Milton was on."

Joan Rivers once asked George if it was true that Milton Berle was very "well endowed." Leaving nothing to the imagination, George replied:

"Yeah, he had a lot from here down. From here down, I need makeup."

Then there was Groucho Marx. Although he liked Groucho, the two had a running feud that revealed itself in various ways. He talks about this in a 1976 *New Yorker* interview:

"I used to sing a song that went, 'If You Can't See Mama Every Night, You Can't See Mama at All.' A good song. When I'm in Beverly Hills . . . I eat lunch most days at the Hillcrest Country Club, and usually Groucho Marx is there. One day he took a line from the song and made it into sea bass. 'If You Can't Sea Bass Every Night, You Can't See Mama at All.' He told me the joke and I laughed the first time, just to be polite, because it wasn't a very funny joke. But Groucho if he likes it will use it eight, ten times in the same city. . . . Whenever we were together, which was just about every day, I avoided sea bass just so I wouldn't have to hear that line.

"Finally, one day I see it on the menu and I decide to have it, and I don't want Groucho to hear. So I whisper to the waiter, 'I'll have the sea bass, please.' And the waiter leans down and says, 'If you can't sea bass every night, you can't see mama at all.' "

Once at a party, Burns and Groucho got into a discussion about who was the funniest comedian in history. George said he thought the funniest comedian was Charlie Chaplin. Groucho shot back that he thought he was. Burns countered with "Well, if you think you're the funniest, then I must be, because I'm funnier than you"—a reply that prompted Groucho not to talk to him for a month.

"One of Groucho's wives was non-Jewish. They had a lovely daughter named Melinda who one day went with her friends to a club that didn't allow Jews. She wasn't allowed to go in the pool. When Groucho found out, he wrote a letter to the president of the club asking, 'Since my daughter is only half Jewish, would it be all right if she went into the pool only up to her waist?' "

He told this yarn to Larry King.

"The Marx Brothers were playing a theater, and their father was in to see the show. And the fellow in back says, 'Harpo Marx is deaf and dumb and can't talk.' The father turns around and says, 'No, no, no. Harpo can talk! The guy says, 'Don't tell me Harpo talks.' The father says, 'I know him better than you know him. He talks!' The guy says, 'I'll bet you twenty-five dollars he doesn't talk.' The father says, 'If you lay me odds, I'll take the bet!' "

George may have had a problem or two with Groucho, but he simply adored Harpo. They played golf together.

"I absolutely hated the game [golf]. I hated it because I was never very good at it. I just enjoyed the company, and I loved to sing while I was on the course. Harpo, on the other hand, was a good golfer."

One time, Harpo's third shot landed in one of the traps around the green.

"Because I didn't want to disturb Harpo or make him nervous, I stayed at the bottom of the hill while he climbed to the top of the hill and got ready to hit the ball out of the trap. Suddenly he looked down at me standing at the bottom of the hill and said, 'What are you doing there, George?' I called back, 'You're one under par. I don't want to upset you by watching you hit out of the trap.' And he said, 'You're upsetting me. Come on up here, like you always do.'

"So I told him okay, and I trudged up the hill and stood at the edge of the trap while he was preparing to strike the ball. I looked the other way so I wouldn't upset him. But then he asked, 'Why aren't you watching me, George, like you always do?' And I explained again, 'Harpo, I don't want to upset you. You're one under par.' And again he said, 'You are upsetting me. Do what you always do.' So just as he took his backswing, I started to sing 'When Irish Eyes Are Smiling' in a very loud voice. And he missed the ball completely, which of course was the end of his under par round. But we stayed friends anyway."

"I liked Harpo. Harpo and Susan adopted four kids. And I said to Harpo and Susan, 'How many kids are you going to adopt?' They said, 'As many as the windows we have in the house.' They were charming people."

George tells of a memorable New Year's Eve party at Harpo's house. About three o'clock in the morning many of his best friends were about to leave:

"We were all standing outside waiting for our cars,

the sky was filled with stars and the air was crisp and we were all together and everybody was feeling wonderful. Then suddenly, from the sky, we heard a clarinet playing a slow, beautiful version of 'Auld Lang Syne.' It was Harpo, standing at an open upstairs window, playing good night to his friends. Nobody said a word. This was a group that couldn't say good morning without doing five minutes, but nobody said a word. And I'll never forget it."

# CHAPTER EIGHT

# Television Days

*"He's been entertaining people forty years and nobody ever knew it."*
—Gracie Allen in *Say Goodnight, Gracie* by Cheryl Blythe (1986)

George and Gracie had a personal life as well. Unable to have children due to Gracie's frail health—she had a congenital heart condition—they adopted two children from The Cradle in Evanston, Illinois. They named the boy Ronnie and the girl Sandra. They were so pleased to become parents, they told their friends Bob and Delores Hope about The Cradle. It was the "in place" for adoptions by Hollywood celebrities. In the ensuing year the Hopes adopted four children from there themselves.

"You'll have to pick them up personally, they don't deliver,' George told Bob Hope. Then later he would joke that "Gracie and I never even got a cut."

Television was sweeping the land in the early fifties, and George and Gracie took another giant leap in their show-biz odyssey: the world of television. By the time he had entered the television arena, George Burns had been entertaining audiences of one sort or another since 1906.

In October 1950 Burns and Allen moved over to television with a biweekly (later a weekly) domestic situation comedy. Burns opened with a monologue and talked to the audience directly reminiscent of the current hit *Seinfeld*. It also provided an early glimpse of the stand-up routine he developed as a solo performer after Gracie left the show. He would take an occasional puff from his cigar and sing lines from songs he never finished.

*The New York Times* quoted George's comment to their first Burns and Allen television show (October 22, 1950):

"We came in without any fanfare. It didn't help when we heard everybody talking about NBC's new comedy star. We talked in vaudeville, we talked in radio, we talked in television. It wasn't that hard to go from one medium to another."

As usual he was on top of every facet of the show. And more than that, he enjoyed it immensely.

"Television's got one thing going for me that no other form ever had. It's this: You're always guessing. That's the exciting thing. Whether you're right or wrong, every week you have a new chance. . . . The guy who has to take a couple of days every week to get away from his business, has a business he ought to get away from permanently.

"I just get good people together and let them do their job. If I can't help them, I leave them alone. . . . If one guy doesn't do his job and pull up the curtain, nobody goes on. Everybody's job is important—each person is part and parcel of the show. We do our show easily. We don't try to get all the laughs. There's very little pressure.

". . . Most performers work hard and fast. When you watch their show, you eat fast. When you eat fast, you get indigestion and don't watch the show again."

George was also quick to grasp the importance of a dollar in making a television show. He was already showing his potential as a producer in the early live shows.

"The fellow who played the part of the insurance adjuster is a movie actor, Charles Lane. He's very expensive. He wanted a thousand to do that bit, but he said he'd do it for a hundred dollars if I'd give him a close-up. If you don't mind it will take only a few seconds. 'Come on, Mr. Lane. Okay, boys, move in. [The camera moves back over to George]. 'That's it, Mr. Lane.' [To audience] I just saved nine hundred dollars and it helps. We're only on every other week."

The television version of *The Burns and Allen Show* had several of the same characters as the radio series. Hal March played neighbor Harry Morton; Gracie's friend, Bea Benadaret, was still playing his wife, Blanche. Bea was appearing on many shows and would have to commute from Los Angeles. She was starting to work on a new series called *I Love Lucy*, with Lucille Ball and her husband, Desi Arnaz. Burns wasn't worried about the conflicting schedules because as he told director Fred De Cordova and writer Paul Henning:

"Fellas, it'll never happen, it just won't work. Here's this red-headed American married to the Cuban. The public won't buy it."

He was dead wrong.

*I Love Lucy* was an enormous success, as was Desilu, their production company. George took a page out of the Desilu song book, and followed suit by organizing his own production company, McFadden Productions, taking the name from his brother Willie's home address at McFadden St. It soon became one of the most efficient production companies in Hollywood.

Founded in 1955, McFadden Corporation filmed television shows and commercials at its headquarters on the General Service Studio lot in the heart of Hollywood. In addition to the *The Burns and Allen Show,* the company also produced for TV *The Bob Cummings Show, The People's Choice,* starring Jackie Cooper, *Mona McClusky,* starring Juliet Prowse, and *Mr. Ed,* starring Alan Young.

His monologues on *The Burns and Allen Show* reflected his no-nonsense production skills.

"In ten minutes, I'm sure Gracie and Blanche will have another scheme. But ten minutes of television time costs lots of money. It might even cost more than a week in Palm Springs. I think I'll save that dough."

George totally enjoyed the new medium of television. He felt that comedy should be directed as if it were drama.

"After Gracie made a joke, the camera would stay on me until I reacted to that joke. Let's say the joke is, 'My brother's coming with pineapples.' Gracie would pick up an ashtray, put it on the table, say the line, and walk away. The camera would show me deadpan.

"Now we show it to the audience. If that line doesn't get a laugh, we put back the piece of film where Gracie picked up the ashtray and put it on the table. Then we put in a very small snicker [on the laugh track] and let it lay an egg.

"If it got a laugh, then my reaction would stay, but if not the camera would follow Gracie."

Any television writer will tell you that comedy is the hardest kind of writing there is. *The Burns and Allen Show* writers had a special task before them.

"Good writers will give you what you want, but if you don't know what you want, they can't give you anything. . . . I've got to get to Palm Springs. My writers are waiting for me. They've been down there for me. They've been there for a week and so far all they've written is my name at the bottom of all the restaurant checks. They need me. I'm the only one who can type."

Years later, as a producer of *The People's Choice,* he would inject a little humor.

"I would read a script, and know something's wrong. But I don't know how to fix it. So I go out to Hillcrest, I wander around the clubhouse until I spot some $250,000 comedy writer.

"I tell him the story. I say it's great. He looks at me like I've got two heads. To show how smart he is, he points out how it can be fixed. Now I've got $250,000 worth of comedy brains for nothing. I go back to the office and call Irv Brecher. I tell him how to fix his scripts, but I don't say where I got my ideas. And everybody tells everybody what a genius I am."

George was continually refining his formats. For example, in 1954 his son, Ronnie, became part of the show. It made good sense. The competitive *Ozzie and Harriet Show* was also a situation comedy about a real-life show-business family. When their real children, David and Ricky Nelson, were brought into the show, its popularity soared.

When asked what Ronnie was really like, George told a reporter for *TV Star Parade:*

"He's charming, he's diplomatic, but you can't always

be sure what he's thinking. And I like that, too. I don't like people whose entire personality is on the surface."

In 1957 George told the *Star Free Press:*

"It doesn't help a series to change locale or bring in a new star. You can bring in new subject matter. We added Ronnie, our son, to the show and it opened up a new subject for stories—the problems of a twenty-year boy. Changes are gradual. We don't wait until the end of a season to change anything. In the middle of a season, we went to Europe. . . . The changes are gradual."

George took another departure from the norm when he jumped aboard the Western bandwagon in the late 1950s. The Westerns dominated prime time with such shows as *Maverick, Wyatt Earp, Gunsmoke, Cheyenne, Wagon Train,* etc. He decided "if we can't wup em, join em'," but keep it funny.

In his opening September 1957 episode, instead of wearing his usual dapper suit and tie, George appeared looking like the original rhinestone cowboy. After a couple of minutes, George stepped aside to explain his unusual attire.

"The situation downstairs has nothing to do with our opening show. . . . We were going to start our new season with a straight Western. That's why I've got this outfit on. This is great. I'm dressed this-a-way, and the plot went that-a-way."

He confessed his ignorance about Western ways to *TV Guide* (September 28, 1957).

"I know very little about being a cowboy. I'm not even sure if you're supposed to saddle Old Paint and ride, or paint an old saddle and ride later when the paint dries."

When George asked Gracie which of her relatives she was going to talk about that night, Gracie was off and running; the cast of characters in her tales included:

Wyatt Allen—a Western town marshal. He was a perfect shot—everyone who shot at him, hit him. He had an all-white stallion named "Old Paint" because that was the color he painted it [the horse].

Cousin Robin Allen—who stole from the rich and gave to the poor. He read someplace that to open a safe, the burglar always sandpapered his fingertips down to where the nail was very sensitive. That's how he got caught. When he touched the dial with those sensitive fingertips, it hurt so much he screamed and woke up the whole neighborhood.

Great-grandfather Daniel Allen—a pioneer and trailblazer. A lot of places in history were named after him. He'd ride up to some Indians and whatever he said, the Indians would give it that name. In Arizona alone, there is the Where-Am-I Mountain, Where-Am-I Canyon, Where-Am-I Creek.

The family tree also included such notables as Scoop Allen—the newspaperman, Hitchcock Allen—the Pony Express rider, and Balzac Allen—the novelist.

*The Burns and Allen Show* was going strong still in 1958. Awards were plentiful and audiences loved it. The TV critics' poll voted George and Gracie the best comedy team over Lucy and Desi. Over the course of their eight-year run, *The Burns and Allen Show* received a total of twelve Emmy nominations—six for Gracie as Best Actress/Comedian, two for Bea Benaderet as Best Supporting Actress, and four for the show itself as Best Comedy Series. In 1957, George ran the following ad in the trades:

## I'M PAYING FOR THIS AD, SO I CAN SAY WHAT I WANT.

I think my wife, GRACIE ALLEN, is a great artist and deserves an Emmy.

My son, RONNIE BURNS, is a promising young actor and should get an award, too . . . next year.

BEA BENADERET deserves an award as Supporting Actress.

LARRY KEATING deserves an award as a Supporting Actor.

HARRY VON ZELL should have gotten an award years ago.

My writers, KEITH FOWLER, HARVEY HELM, NORMAN PAUL, and WILLIE BURNS, should get an award.

ROD AMATEAU, my director/producer, should get . . . two awards.

As for me, I'm pathetic. Vote for Jack Benny.

GEORGE BURNS

Unfortunately, critics and viewers don't get to vote for their choice in the Emmys. The results were the same as they had been in previous years: not one winner.

In 1958, Gracie Allen decided to call it a career. As early as 1955 she indicated to the *Los Angeles Examiner* (January 23, 1955) that the strain was starting to get to her. "I'll say one thing, and I'll say it right out loud," she said. "I liked television better when I did a live show every two weeks. It gave me a breather. Now we film the show, but I have to do it every week. I think I felt fresher when I had a little time to myself."

# CHAPTER NINE

# George Without Gracie

*"I'm happy and flattered to appear on one
of George's shows.
Also I am curious. Burns without Allen?
What can he pay me?"*
—Jack Benny, cited in *Say Goodnight, Gracie*

By 1958 Gracie still looked young and vigorous. The
sad truth, however, was that she wasn't. She had suffered
a prolonged series of chest pains, and was diagnosed as
having had a mild heart attack. Her chronic migraine
headaches, at least, were tolerable. Now she was con-
fronted with a life-threatening situation. In an era before
bypass surgery and angiograms, she was given a prescription for nitroglycerin tablets and told to relax as much as
possible.

On June 4, 1958, George and Gracie filmed the
229th and final episode of *The Burns and Allen
Show*. They would never work together professionally
again.

The last episode of their show was aired on June 14,
1958. According to *Life* magazine, George gave the following response to Gracie's retirement:

"Maybe after six months one of the kids will spill a

glass of milk on her. Then maybe she'll retire from the kids, too."

But *Time* (March 3, 1958) gave a different account of the circulating rumors about Gracie's impending retirement. George told the *Time* reporter:

"I didn't blame her. She spent all her time worrying about wardrobe, makeup, getting her hair done at rehearsals. And after we got into television, learning thirty to forty new pages of dialogue every week.

"No one so richly deserves it [retirement]. Her kind of work takes a lot out of you. Like I ask Gracie how her brother is and she talks for four minutes without stopping. That's very hard work. I can always keep busy both as an executive and a performer."

Yet he added some typical Burns levity.

"When Gracie retired, I went into show business. I was retired the whole time I worked with her. When I worked with Gracie I didn't have to do anything. My big lines were, 'You don't say,' and, 'Oh, really!' Things like that. I had the talent off the stage, and she had it on. I couldn't do what I thought of, Gracie could."

And what made them work so well together?

"I believe in what I'm doing, and Gracie believed in what she did. I don't think it works if you don't believe in it, in any business. I don't care what you do for a living. You can make felt hats for a living. And if you enjoy making them they'll turn out to be very good felt hats. But if you hate what you're doing and you got to get up out of bed in the morning and make felt hats, they'll be bad felt hats. They won't fit. I would rather be a failure at something I'm in love with than be successful in something I hate."

And George did just that. He stayed with something

he loved, and on February 20, 1958, he announced plans for a new pilot. It would be the same genre, but this time without Gracie as its focal point. Not surprisingly, it was called *The George Burns Show*. For George Burns it was business as usual—that "show must go on" philosophy. He told *Variety:*

"If they like my pilot, that's fine. If they don't, I'll start smoking smaller cigars. At sixty-two, I'm too old to retire."

The show seemed like a natural. It had all the original cast, minus Gracie. He arranged for such well-known guest stars as Bob Cummings, Phyllis Kirk, Peter Lawford, Carol Channing, and of course his old pal, Jack Benny. Always on the lookout for new talent, people like actress Suzanne Pleshette, poet/singer Rod McKuen, and actress Mary Moore—she was not yet Mary Tyler Moore.

George was pleased with what he had put together, and said as much to *TV Guide* (October 25, 1958):

"We can go anywhere with this format, do anything, use almost any guest star perfectly legitimately. In fact when Gracie saw the pilot film she turned to me and said, 'You know, I didn't miss me at all.' Nobody did, because nobody had ever been accustomed to seeing Gracie in these new surroundings. . . . [But] if an imitator were to come along, the audience would miss her more than ever."

*The George Burns Show* premiered on October 21, 1958, on NBC. For the first time in thirty-five years George Burns was alone in the spotlight. His timing was sharp, he was funny, but without Gracie the heart was gone. The show just didn't work for the audience. It was canceled after a single season.

Gracie's condition was worsening. She was now in bed much of the time with two nurses by her side. George was almost retirement age and had more money than he could ever spend. McFadden Productions was a lucrative enterprise, and would remain so for many years. The problem was what to do.

He may have been down, but he surely wasn't out. To quit was not his style. Show business was the blood of George Burns. He told Roy Leonard of WGN Radio in Chicago:

"The minute you walk out there and the audience stands up, you get a lot of energy. And you're tired and you're full of booze a little bit. But the minute you walk out, the music plays and the audience stands up, and the love comes over the footlights. And I've been around for a lot of years, and there's one thing I believed in, and it works for me. And it will work for you, too. You can't help getting older, but you don't have to get old.

"No, I don't think anybody should quit no matter what they do. I don't think anybody should ever retire. Nobody. As a matter of fact, if I went into business I would hire all people over seventy. They would do a wonderful job, because they know their business. They made their mistakes, and it would be a very successful business.' "

"Even if you can't live in the past, it's nice to have one. I'll tell you. I was very, very fortunate, and I think the kids today can be, too. Fall in love with something you think has a future. I don't care if you want to be a cutter of ladies' dresses, or you want to be a singer."

After a preliminary engagement at Harrah's in Lake Tahoe, Nevada—hardly big time—George opened at the Sahara Hotel in Las Vegas in midsummer 1959. He took the De Castro Sisters and a young singer named Bobby Darin with him as an opening act. He had discovered Darin, soon to be a big-time star, singing "Mack the Knife" on *The Ed Sullivan Show.* He telephoned his brother Willie immediately. "Grab him. I don't care what you do, grab him."

Admittedly he was nervous. But he revised his memory into comic material.

"I was drinking a lot . . . I set up two glasses backstage—one with sand for my soft shoe, and the other with scotch. Reaching for a drink, I gulped down the sand.

"If you've got material that you think is funny but the audience doesn't, you don't use it again. . . . And if an act is *too* smart for an audience, that means it isn't funny."

In 1962 George told Jack Paar how he felt entertaining in Las Vegas with the likes of Judy Garland and Harry Belafonte.

"It didn't make me nervous because all of us singers have the same style. Judy sits down at the edge of the stage and sings 'Over the Rainbow.' Belafonte opens his shirt. I tried both styles. It didn't work. I opened my shirt and I sat down. I not only couldn't get up, I caught cold."

"Judy Garland was a great talent. I remember her when she was a child. Louis B. Mayer was head of MGM and discovered her. She was a smash. She was twelve years old. The same thing happened to me except for one thing. When I was twelve, Louis B. Mayer was twelve."

The later fifties and early sixties were clearly not the best of times for George. He could still draw a crowd, but it was obvious that there was not the same kind of demand for a singer in his seventies with an undiluted vaudeville style. He tried to create another team for himself, working at one point or another with Madeline Kahn, Bernadette Peters, Ann-Margret, and Carol Channing. His routine was somewhere between a single and a double. He'd start with a monologue, sing a few songs, let his actress/partner do a few songs, then close with some Burns and Allen routine.

He even tried a new TV series called *Wendy and Me* with a perky and bright young actress named Connie Stevens. Set in a Southern California apartment house, the show premiered on September 14, 1964, with Connie Stevens playing a slightly fuzzy, mixed-up young bride married to an airline pilot, and George as the owner of the building. The show closed just one year later, the last episode being aired on September 6, 1965. George mused over the fact years later in a *TV Guide* interview (September 15, 1984):

"The problem was competition. Andy Williams was on one channel, and he sang better than I did. And the other channel was Lucille Ball, who was a smash. It's bad enough being up against Andy Williams and Lucille Ball, but to have to fight with color, too, we didn't have a chance."

# CHAPTER TEN

# A New Direction

*The other day I had a date with a girl about 25.*
*I shaved and showered. Put on some cologne,*
*a nice shirt, and a tie. I looked up in the mirror*
*and I looked so good that I said, "Wait a minute.*
*That kid's too old for me."*
—George Burns, *Stars Salute Israel at 30,*
ABC (May 8, 1978)

George's world was taken from him when Gracie died on August 27, 1964. Three years earlier Gracie had suffered a severe heart attack. The night she died George had come home from the studio tired, yet with an enthusiastic feeling about his new series *(Wendy and Me)*. Shortly after dinner she began feeling chest pains and when she did not respond to her pills, George rushed her to Cedars of Lebanon Hospital. She was admitted at 10:25 P.M. At 11:15 she was gone. George was at her side. Gracie Allen was fifty-eight years old.

The news of Gracie's death was on the front page of *The New York Times,* and the *Los Angeles Times.* In one of its rare headlines above the paper's logo, news of her death was announced:

## "RADIO-TV COMEDIENNE
## GRACE ALLEN, 58, DIES.
## HUSBAND-PARTNER GEORGE BURNS
## AT BEDSIDE . . ."

Gracie's funeral was held at the Church of the Recessional at Forest Lawn Cemetery. Among the pallbearers were Jack Benny, George Jessel, Edward G. Robinson, and Mervyn LeRoy. The funeral service was described in *Variety*:

"George Jessel spoke for all biz in his brief eulogy at the service . . . Jessel, a lifetime friend of both Gracie and George Burns . . . paid the highest tribute to the talent of the comedienne saying . . . , 'The act is over, the bow music has faded, the billing will have to be changed . . . the next stage manager will have to be told 'George N. Burns, is one and alone.' "

George was devastated by Gracie's death. But his public persona was one of calm, and intermittent humor.

"Whenever Gracie got a heart attack, I'd give her the pill. She'd put it under her tongue until it would dissolve. And I'd hold her until she got well. [The night she died] the doctor was in there, and he came back and he said, 'She's gone.' So I went in—I went to see her. I told her—I said, 'How can you do it? I got a pocketful of pills, you know.' "

At the funeral he was approached by Herb Brower, his longtime chief of production. Herb Brower told George that of all the female stars he had worked with, Gracie was the only one who was a real lady. George made a revealing admission.

"Yes, she was. . . . You know that I wasn't a true-blue husband. But I loved Gracie. And we were always together in the evenings. I always came home. I made sure to be there. We would go to bed together, and every night we would lie in bed, holding hands and watching television.

"For months I couldn't sleep. I couldn't adjust to her not being there next to me. Then one night—I can't explain it—I was about to get into bed, but instead I pulled back the covers on Gracie's bed and got in it. I slept like a baby and I've been sleeping there ever since."

He began a practice of visiting Gracie at Forest Lawn at least once a month. In a *60 Minutes* segment, he visited her crypt with Ed Bradley.

"I still talk to her all the time. I hope she hears me. If she does, it makes me feel good. You see, Gracie made everything possible for me. I don't think you'd be interviewing me if it wasn't for Gracie. . . . I wouldn't have this house. I wouldn't be sitting here. I don't know where I'd be. I didn't do well from eight to twenty-seven, and from twenty-seven to ninety-two, I'm doing fine."

He added a touch of humor for writer Rita Christopher in a 1977 article for *Macleans:*

"Oh yes, I visit Gracie about every two weeks, just to tell her what I'm doing. I don't know if she hears me, but I've got nothing to lose. And it gives me new material. I know all her neighbors. On the right is Alan Ladd, on the left is Jeanette MacDonald."

George buried his grief in the only way he knew how; he devoted himself to his only other love—his work. He took the plunge once again.

"What am I going to do? Go into the dress business?

When Gracie gave it up, I thought it was the end of me. I sat around two or three years. It's no good for you. You must do something. I was semi-retired. Did only a few things I liked doing. Money didn't enter into it. If I didn't enjoy it, I wouldn't do it, although they'd pay me a bundle."

And work there was. His production company co-produced the television series *No Time for Sergeants,* based on the hit Broadway play. At the same time he toured the country playing nightclub and theater engagements with such diverse partners as Carol Channing, Jane Russell, Dorothy Provine, Connie Haynes, and Berle Davis. He also embarked on a series of solo concerts, playing university campuses, New York Philharmonic, ending up a successful season at Carnegie Hall, where he enthralled a capacity audience with his show-stopping songs, dances, and jokes.

Singing was something he still enjoyed immensely.

"I started to sing when I was seven. I fell in love with it, and I'm still in love with it. And don't forget that until I was twenty-seven years old, I didn't do well.

"You think my voice is like the tearing of a dishrag? Wrong. I'd rather sing than do almost anything. I was married to Gracie for thirty-eight years. Every night, I'd sing her six, seven songs till she fell asleep. I did that for thirty years. After you're married thirty years and you're in bed with your wife, I found it's a lot easier to just sing."

And so when other men were thinking retirement, George Burns, former vaudeville performer, and radio and TV straight man, embarked on a new career.

Seventy-one-year-old George Burns opened at the

Riviera Hotel in Las Vegas in May 1967. He made his entrance with a puff of cigar smoke blown from the wings. Much of his newfound appeal rested with how he marketed his age. No one ever did it better. His opening line said it all: "I get a standing ovation just standing."

He feels that today's entertainers don't have to pay their proper dues, and make too much too soon.

"Kids today make it too fast with TV and the millions who see them. Me, what did I know? I started show business at seven. It took me a long time to get discovered. Young kids can learn from this. They gotta hang in there. But if they don't hit it by seventy-seven then they should go into another business.

"A lot of people practice getting old. They start to walk slower and they hold on to things. They start practicing when they are seventy, and when they are seventy-five, they're a hit. They've made it. They are now old. Who the hell wants that?"

George Burns was working Vegas now, but between appearances there was little else to do. He began dating. Among those he started to see were actress Evelyn Keyes, a Los Angeles woman named Lita Baron, and twenty-year-old Lisa Miller, who was a member of the "Kids Next Door" group who had opened for him in Las Vegas. Although Lisa would later say that they made love every night for three years, George chose to respect the usual moral code.

"Now hold on, I know what you are thinking! I admit I was thinking the same thing, but it didn't happen that way."

Yet the persona had been established of the seventy-plus-year-old man who wined, dined, and courted young women. And he always kept you guessing. On the *Stars Salute Israel at 30* special aired on ABC on May 8, 1978, he pursued his role of the aging rake: "Imagine Israel is thirty years old—I have a grandson who's sixty-five.

"I get a lot of mail. People always ask me the same question. 'Why do you go out with young girls?' Look, I'd go out with women my own age, but I understand Golda Meir is not a good dancer and Helen Hayes doesn't boogie, and Lillian Gish can't sing harmony. So I'm stuck with these beautiful young girls.

"I usually take them to a good restaurant. I get a table in a nice corner so they can do their homework. If they get all A's I take them out again. If they flunk, I take out their mothers."

The year 1974 was a difficult one for George, but also an auspicious one. On August 9, he underwent a triple bypass. At age seventy-eight, he was the oldest person to date to have bypass surgery. That same year his older sister Goldie passed away. He was very close to her, and her death left him the remaining member of his immediate family. But the hardest blow of all was the death of his best friend, Jack Benny. George was depleted emotionally.

"My best friend was gone, careerwise I wasn't in great demand, and I wasn't getting any younger. [It was] one of the low points in my life."

In a barely audible voice he spoke at the funeral.

"I don't know if I'll be able to do this. I told Mary I might not be able to do it, but she said, 'Do it, George, you've got to do it.' So I'm going to try but it won't be easy. You are all Jack's friends, but he was something very special to me. He was my closest friend. I knew him for fifty-five years, and I can't imagine my life without Jack Benny. . . . I'll miss him. . . . I'll miss him very much. . . ."

# CHAPTER ELEVEN

# An Oscar for George

*"That movie turned it around for me."*
—Cited in *Macleans* (August 20, 1977)

Then came *The Sunshine Boys,* the role of Al Lewis, and an Oscar at the age of seventy-nine. Ironically, the role of Al Lewis was written for Jack Benny. George again was philosophical.

"Thinking about what Benny would have done didn't affect my performance one way or another. Look, death is the only exit for all of us. You know in vaudeville when you were canceled, the manager would come around and give you your pictures back. That's how you knew you were through, before he even said anything. Well, in life we all get our pictures back sometime.

"I'm perfect for the [Al Lewis] part. They're looking for an old Jewish vaudevillian, and I'm an old vaudevillian.

"The character of Al Lewis fits me like a glove. . . . I felt the character of Al Lewis so strongly that Monday morning. At the time I said to myself, 'If I'm a hit as Al Lewis, I might never go back to being George Burns again. I'll let somebody else with less talent play him.

"*The Sunshine Boys* was great. Walter Matthau is a

great actor. And Dick Benjamin. Herb Ross, the director, Neil Simon, the writer. I love acting. It's easy to do. You sit down and you can act. You don't have to stand up all the time. On the stage you walk out there and you stand there. If you asked me to get up there and stand for an hour, I couldn't do it. But with the audience out there, and they applaud and their love comes through the footlights and gives you vitality, you can stand. If I can sit and get paid, I'm in the right business. I won an Academy Award."

Burns took to the acting like the proverbial duck to water, or so he says: "[Acting] is much easier than what I've always done. You don't have to remember anything to begin with. If you play Vegas you've got about an hour by yourself. You have to remember every cue, every song, every lyric. If it's no good, you can't do it again. That can't happen. The director says, 'Come in,' and you walk in. If you stay out in the hall, you're a bad actor. If your director says, 'Sit down,' you sit down. It's nice to be able to sit down anyway at my age."

"I had always heard that the toughest thing about acting was being able to laugh and being able to cry. I say, 'Nonsense!' If I am doing a scene in which I'm supposed to cry, all I do is think of my sex life. I must really be a hell of an actor. This morning after taking a shower, I looked at myself in the mirror and laughed and cried at the same time."

He also showed himself to be master at explaining why a certain scene wouldn't work. He mentioned the problem to costar Walter Matthau.

"Listen, this sketch will never work. . . . It won't work because the props are funny . . . you can't play a funny dialogue against funny props. People won't know whether to watch the props or listen to the dialogue."

*The Sunshine Boys* opened up a whole new career for George. It was his first film role since *Honolulu* in 1939, and gained him a well-deserved Oscar as Best Supporting Actor for 1975. The four other nominees for Best Supporting Actor that year were Brad Dourif *(One Flew Over the Cuckoo's Nest)*, Burgess Meredith *(The Day of the Locust)*, Chris Sarandon *(Dog Day Afternoon)*, and Jack Warden *(Shampoo)*. As Ben Johnson and Linda Blair announced the winner, George made his way to the podium amid loud approval from the audience. Recalling that this was his first film since 1939, he announced:

"This is all so exciting. I've decided to keep making one movie every thirty-six years. You get to be new again."

Then he told reporters: "I'm thinking of taking on Gentile roles and becoming the new Robert Redford. . . . I'm going home to have a bowl of soup—barley soup."

In 1978 George (then eighty-two) and his current leading lady, thirteen-year-old Brook Shields, presented the Best Supporting Actress Oscar to Maggie Smith for *California Suite,* which, like *The Sunshine Boys,* was written by Neil Simon.

"That's when I became an actor. I had always used the name George Burns, but in that picture it was the first time I played a character."

When *The Sunshine Boys* was released in November 1975 it broke the single-day box office record at New York City's Radio Music Hall. The roles started to pour in. In 1977 he was given the title role in *Oh, God!* Then came *Sergeant Pepper's Lonely Hearts Club Band, Just You and Me, Kid* with Brooke Shields, *Going in Style* with Art Carney and Lee Strasberg, *Oh, God! Book II,* and *Oh, God! You Devil!*

In no movie was he more popular than *Oh, God!* George offers some interesting observations. This is what he told Larry King:

"Anything I do at my age is a miracle. The first God! movie was good. That's 'cause John Denver was good. It was good casting. If God came down and looked for a nice man, he'd have picked John Denver. I don't think the picture would have worked if instead of John Denver we had Milton Berle."

He offered this observation to Roy Leonard:

"The nice thing about playing God is that nobody has ever seen him, so they don't know whether I'm good or bad. They asked me to play God, and I called up all my friends and said, 'How do you play God?' And nobody knew how to play God. So I just believed the words. . . ."

Burns had a definite idea as to what God should be like:

"He should be kind, wise, witty, sympathetic, and he could use more humorous epigrams. He shouldn't be ethnic and use words like schtick and schlock." Just like George himself.

"One day I was playing bridge at the club and a kid called and asked for God. He had seen me in the movie and wanted me to make it stop raining."

George talks to Roy Leonard about two of his other films, *Oh, God! Book II* (1980) and *Going in Style* (1979):

"In *Oh, God! Book II,* things are bad. I look down and

you hear me talking, but you don't see me. And I come down to a Chinese restaurant where John Denver always eats on Saturdays. He has lunch there. I thought it would be nice to see John Denver again. And while I'm in the Chinese restaurant, I hear a little girl say something. They don't see me but they know I'm there by my voice.

"And she says, 'Sometimes you've got to believe in things you can't see.' And it sort of catches me. I decide I'll see John Denver some other time. And when her father goes out and she's left with a fortune cookie, she opens up the fortune cookie and it says, 'I'd like to see you in the ladies' lounge,' and it's signed, 'God!'

"She picks it up and throws it away. Then she picks up the other one and it says, 'Yeah, Tracy, I mean you!' And it's signed, 'God!' She comes in and I talk to her. She's a little eleven-year-old girl who's a marvelous actress. Her name's Louanne, and she just finished playing *Annie* here. She's a great little natural actress, and I think we've got a fine movie here."

On *Going in Style:*

"The person who gets credit for that film is the director, Martin Brest. He's twenty-seven years old and he took three old guys—myself, Lee Strasberg, and Art Carney. I'm eight-three, Lee Strasberg is seventy-six, and Art Carney, who was the kid at sixty-one. And we're directed by this young fellow who not only directed it, he wrote it. Carney is great. He's a fine actor and very funny. Lee Strasberg—he's a great teacher."

George's career took on a fifth dimension in 1980. He became a recording artist with a country-and-western album entitled "I Wish I Was Eighteen Again," for Mercury/Polygram. He followed that with an second album, "George Burns in Nashville," and then a third called "Young at Heart." His rendition of the title song was so touching that it was included on the sound track of a two-reel documentary short of the same name. It captured an Oscar for Best Documentary of a Short Subject, and is about two people who find love and marriage in their eighties.

And how did George feel about becoming a country artist at age eighty-four? He thought it was quite appropriate.

'Why not! After all, I'm older than most countries."

During a discussion with Roy Leonard about making the album, he says:

"I was in Vegas doing *Going in Style*. We were just finishing the movie. And Sunny Throckmorton wrote a song, "I Wish I Was Eighteen Again." And he went to Mercury Records. He went to one of the executives and says, 'Charlie, I've got a great song.' Well, he plays it and Charlie says, 'How old are you, Sunny?' Sunny says, 'I'm forty years old.' He says, 'You're too young to sing that song. Who can we get to sing it? Let's get the oldest!' They looked around; they couldn't find Moses, so they got me. Charlie came to Vegas and played it for me. I love to sing so they asked me to come to Nashville. I told them to get the tickets and I went.

"I think the whole album was good. I'll tell you why. In the first place I had nothing to do with that. That's made in Nashville. And the musicians are the greatest. The arrangers are the greatest. And the country/western/ pop and those kind of songs are wonderful words. They tell great stories. They're sad when they were supposed to be sad. When they're supposed to be funny, they're funny. It's nice to sing them, because you've got that great music.

" 'I Wish I Was Eighteen Again,' the whole album is for me—just imagine this—thirty-two violins, six guitars, bass and drums, and eight backup singers. With all that help, they didn't need me. They could have used Dolly Parton."

After the Oscar and subsequent movies, Burns said to Walter Matthau:

"Can you imagine this happening to me? I was never this big in the days with Gracie."

When asked to comment on rumors about a movie on his life, Burns replied wryly, "They may. But they can't find an actor old enough to play me."

# CHAPTER TWELVE

# A League of His Own

*"It's easy to look good at my age. I wear a turtleneck, which cuts out the wrinkles on my neck. And I got trunks full of hair. I got one trunk with just parts in the middle. When I go to sleep, my trunks look better than I do."*
—Cited in *New York Post* (March 11, 1996)

Since Jack Benny's death, Irving Fine had been George's manager. Writer Hal Goldman, who like Fine had been in the Benny camp, was also working for George. Both were among the best in the business. Did George ever mind all the attention he was getting?

"Do I *mind* it? Of course not. I love it. This is show business and I'm George Burns. If they stopped over and said, 'Hello, Sam Newman,' it would bother me a little. People say, 'When are you going to retire, George?' I say, 'I am retired—you think show business is work.'"

Playing Carnegie Hall was a little like coming full circle—you got to start over without some of the inconveniences:

"I'm only playing Carnegie Hall because the Jefferson Theater on Fourteenth Street wasn't available. Actually the reason I'm playing here is because if you're old enough you get to be new. When you play Carnegie Hall you don't have to have a good memory."

He was harsh on those who force people to retire at sixty-five or seventy.

"Let me tell you something. In the first place there is a law that you have to quit when you're seventy. When I was seventy-seven I started a new career. I became an actor. I won an Academy Award. Since then I've made three or four pictures. And here at eighty-four, I'm now a country singer."

He echoed the same sentiments nine years later.

"Age is a state of mind, an attitude. I see people that the minute they get to be sixty, they start practicing to be old. They start taking little steps. They drop food on themselves. They take little naps when you are talking to them. By the time they're seventy, they've made it. They're now a hit. They're old. Not me . . . I like young people. I don't think it's good when older people just hang around each other comparing gravy stains . . . unless it's expensive gravy. And I'm not interested in yesterday . . . I'm ninety-three and I love my age.

When he was honored by NBC for his eighty years in show business, on September 9, 1983, he remembered his parents.

"I only wish my mother and father were here. My father would be a hundred and sixty-seven and my mother would be a hundred and forty-three. My father liked young girls, too."

"I love old age. I never leave home without it."

He talked to Roy Leonard about working with such contemporary acts as the Bee Gees and Peter Frampton.

"I was amazed when I met them. They told me that when Peter Frampton was twenty-four years old he made $52 million. That he had one album that sold sixty million and he got $3 an album, so right there is $48 million. Then I guess he made the other $4 million on just a Sunday concert or something. So Peter Frampton paid his manager that year more than Al Jolson made in his lifetime. . . . When you make $52 million you can go into show business for one year and quit, buy yourself a country, and become a king."

He also recalled a trip he and Gracie took to Russia, years and years ago.

"A long time ago before Hitler was in power, we were forced to go to Russia. We didn't want to go to Russia at the time, but we wanted to shock our friends. So instead of going to Altoona, we went to Russia.

"It's a true story. We wanted to see the Russian Ballet, but the ballet was out of town. We paid for seventeen days, we only stayed three, and we tried to get back our money. We never got back a dime. Jack Pearl's wife, Winnie, was with us. It cost us a fortune, and we came back. We missed the whole thing. The three of us paid ninety-nine dollars a day for three people, which was a fortune in those days. Today for ninety-nine dollars you get a cup of coffee."

George also attended his first Passover Seder in more than half a century at the home of comedian Jan Murray and his wife, Toni. He told Murray how in his day the older comedians tried to hide their Jewishness. For George, in fact, the name Nathan Birnbaum immediately stamped him as Jewish. Jews weren't too popular in George's Irish neighborhood at the turn of the century.

"I haven't been to a Seder since I was five years old back on the East Side with my grandfather. . . . In that generation it was important to appear Gentile. It was tough to be on radio or television if you had a Jewish 'thing' about you. They wouldn't say it. They would say that you were too *New York*. But that was what they meant."

And he continued to work. In addition to doing hit songs, albums, and doing television specials with the likes of Johnny Carson, Bob Hope, Ann-Margret, Goldie Hawn, and others, he also became a best-selling author. Collaborating with both David Fisher and Hal Goldman, George wrote ten books, two of which, *Dr. Burns' Prescription for Happiness* and *Gracie: A Love Story*, were on *The New York Times* best-sellers list for eighteen and twenty weeks, respectively.

He continued to sell out theaters and night clubs, including three or four appearances a year at Caesar's Palace in Las Vegas since 1984. The management at Caesar's signed him to a lifetime contract with the hotel, including an agreement to do a show on the evening of his 100th birthday on January 20, 1996.

He told writer Arthur Marx about it:

"Altogether it's a two-hour show. Someone else opens the show, and I do the second half. I'm onstage for an hour. I do an hour of stand-up. Actually, I do ten minutes standing up and fifty minutes sitting in a chair. Oh, occasionally, I stand up again to do a dance or put over a song. But mostly I sit down. A great invention, sitting down."

Shows yes! But movies were a thing of the past. The reason is simple: At his age it was difficult to remember lines for an entire movie script.

"I already know the jokes and songs I'm going to sing. I've been doing them for fifty years in theaters. Invite me to your house and dinner and I'll do them in your living room, too. But only if you let me smoke a cigar."

And he continued to rail against retirement.

"The happiest people I know are the ones who are still working. The saddest are the ones who are retired. Very few performers retire on their own. It's usually because no one wants them. Six years ago, Sinatra announced his retirement. He's still working."

But there were still realities to be dealt with. He had been a member of the Hillcrest Country Club for nearly sixty years. But the lunch table had emptied out appreciably. Gone were Jolson and Cantor; Harpo and Groucho; Jessel and Jack Benny; Lou Holtz, the Ritz Brothers, Danny Thomas, and Danny Kaye. The whole gang. George Burns was the round table's sole survivor.

"All my friends from radio are gone. I'm not going to die again. I died in Altoona. I don't believe in doing things that have been done. . . . Everything has a price, however. With old age, it means losing so many of the people who meant so much to you."

In 1994, Arthur Marx asked George one final question to close his interview: "Do you miss your friends at Hillcrest?" George was pensive, puffing on his cigar thoughtfully for a moment before answering.

"Yes, I do. I guess that makes me the funniest one at the round table."

He continued to visit Gracie regularly at Forest Lawn; he did his own driving until he was ninety-three, when his chauffeur Conrad took over.

"I was a lousy driver when I was thirty-three . . . I not only went too fast, but my mind was always on shows and scripts. I was constantly making left turns while I was signaling right turns. But at least in those days I could see over the steering wheel. By ninety-three, I had shrunk quite a lot. My car was known as the phantom Cadillac. People could see it whizzing by and they would swear there was no driver.

"Look, who am I kidding? I kept driving because I wouldn't admit to myself that I had become too old to do it. It's a thing called male pride. I can't give up working today. The only difference is that I can't kill anybody if a joke misfires."

Two weeks after announcing plans for a 100th birthday party at Caesar's Palace the entire booking was sold out. It was the earliest sellout in the history of show business according to Irving Fein. There is every indication he planned to make the party, too. He had his opening line.

"It's nice to be here. When you're 100 years old, it's nice to be anywhere."

He told Arthur Marx in the interview for the story that appeared in the winter 1994 edition of *Cigar Aficionado* that he was optimistic:

"I'm in good health . . . knock wood. I'm doing what I love to do and I lead a clean life. I get up every morning. I have a little breakfast. I eat a dish of prunes. I walk around my pool fifteen times for exercise. Then I get dressed, and Conrad drives me to the office here. I stay until twelve. Then I go to Hillcrest and have a little soup. I play bridge until three. I go home and take a nap. I get up around five. . . . Then I have a couple of martinis and smoke a cigar. Maybe I'll go out with my friends . . . Barry Mirkin . . . Irving Brecher and his wife . . . to Chasen's or some other fancy restaurant. Or maybe, I'll go to a friend's house. Of course, I haven't many friends left whose houses I can go to anymore.

"I find you have to take each day as it comes and be thankful for who's left and whatever you can still do. I have my daughter, Sandra, and my son, Ronnie. I have seven grandchildren and five great-grandchildren. They keep me busy and so does my work. Without that, I'd be lost. That's why I'm so grateful that after all these years there's still a demand for me."

# CHAPTER THIRTEEN

# The Final Curtain

*"When the man shows up at the door to return
the pictures, you've got to go."*
—George Burns (at 93), comment to a CBS reporter
on the death of Lucille Ball in 1989

*"When the guy knocks on my door with the pictures,
I'm not going to answer."*
—George Burns (still 93),
P.S. on a letter to William Safire,
*New York Times Magazine,* June 18, 1989

George Burns never made that 100th birthday party.
In July 1994 he stepped out of his bathtub, fell or
blacked out, and suffered a mild concussion. He never
fully recovered. Two months later he was admitted to
Cedars-Sinai Medical Center for surgery to drain fluid
from the surface of his brain. He suffered a heart attack
and a mild stroke on the operating table. He started to
fail badly. A severe bout with the flu prevented him
from attending a party in his honor at the Four Seasons
Hotel in Beverly Hills.

On January 20, 1996, George Burns turned one hundred years old. Time was running out on an American
legend. He would survive his hundredth birthday by

seven weeks and six days. Back in 1964, when Gracie died, George arranged for Episcopal rites, although she was a Roman Catholic. Years later he explained why:

"I want to be buried with Gracie, and since I am Jewish, I can't be buried in Catholic consecrated ground. I hope the Episcopal rites were the right compromise."

George Burns died in his home in Beverly Hills on Saturday morning, March 9, 1996. He had been in show business for ninety-three years. He was survived by two children, seven grandchildren, and five great-grandchildren.

He was laid to rest beside Gracie in Forest Lawn Cemetery, Glendale. Some of Hollywood's brightest and longest-lasting stars—Walter Matthau, Jack Klugman, Jack Lemmon, Milton Berle, and Tony Randall—attended the private service, along with his son, Ronnie, and his daughter, Sandy.

The homages poured in and the memories poured out to extol the life of George Burns, and to mourn the end of an era. Actress Carol Channing, who performed a live act with George for two years in the early 1960s, said she had no doubt he died a happy trouper. "When he went, he thought: 'I did it right to the last minute with my boots on.' That's every actor's wish."

Eighty-seven year-old Milton Berle, who had shared so many wonderful times with George over the years, said that George was probably 'Up there in heaven speaking to St. Peter and doing one-liners on him.

"To me, he's still living. He's still one of my favorites. I think we've lost a heavyweight, an icon. There will never be another one like George Burns."

President Bill Clinton spoke for an entire nation, saying that George Burns' "sense of timing and captivating smile touched the hearts and funnybones of more than three generations.

"He enabled us to see humor in the toughest of times and laugh together as a nation. We will miss him greatly."

George's longtime friend ninety-two year-old Bob Hope summed up the feelings of a lifetime: ". . . I never thought a hundred years was so short a time."

Perhaps the *New York Post* best expressed the gratitude of an entire nation. On Monday, March 11, the following words in large bold print emblazoned across the page. It said it all:

BYE, GEORGE—YOU WERE ONE
OF THE GREATS.

The man finally knocked on the door to return the pictures. This time George had his bags packed.

# EPILOGUE

# Curtain Down

In 1988, George Burns was booked for a single engagement on a holiday weekend. The site was the famous Concord Resort in New York's Catskill Mountains. He still was vintage George Burns. He shuffled out to the center of the stage, his trademark cigar in hand, to the usual standing ovation.

He took his usual bows at the end of the performance; however, this time something unusual happened. An executive of the hotel walked onstage and told George that he believed an old friend of his was in the audience. George peered into the darkened room, taking a familiar puff on his cigar.

The hotel executive said to George, "You once were in a team with a man named Billy Lorraine!"

George was startled, one of the few times in public that he was nonplused. And it showed. His eyes widened behind his glasses, as the old man made his way down the aisle toward the stage.

For almost a year George Burns and Billy Lorraine had been partners. In fact, the act of "Burns and Lorraine" was just breaking up when George Burns met Gracie Allen. They had been small-time vaudeville performers then. Now the old man walking down the aisle was the same Billy Lorraine. They had not seen each other in sixty-five years, since the winter of 1923 in Union City, New Jersey, to be exact.

George had told many jokes and delivered many a monologue about those "good old days." Now he was deeply moved, but never lost his composure. He turned to the piano player and asked him to play "Seems Like Old Times." There were no impressions like in the old days. Each man sang for himself. According to a good friend, it was one of the most emotional nights of his life. Two years later, his old partner Billy Lorraine was dead.

By 1996 George had outlasted the pack. He was the last lion of the old guard, the great comedians who lunched together at a corner table in the Men's Grill known to other members of Hillcrest as the comedians' round table. They were the kings of comedy, a brilliant array of unsurpassed talent and entertainment.

George Burns had become the elder statesman by default. Jolson, Cantor, the Marx Brothers, the Ritz Brothers, Georgie Jessel, Jack Benny, most were now long gone. So were younger members Danny Kaye and Danny Thomas; and the other greats of comedy and vaudeville like Jimmy Durante, Sophie Tucker, Fred Allen, Fannie Bryce, and Blossom Seeley. George, the elder statesman, was holding court virtually alone.

While George grieved for them all, the death of Jack Benny hit him the hardest. According to Herbert Ross, who directed George in *The Sunshine Boys*, George never learned to deal with Jack Benny's death. The two first met in 1921. Jack was seeing the beautiful Mary Kelly, who was living at the Coolidge Hotel on Forty-seventh Street in New York with two other actresses, named Renee Arnold and Gracie Allen. The two young comics liked each other from the start and embraced a friendship that would last more than fifty years.

In later years George worked assiduously with former president Gerald Ford, Irving Fein, and others to persuade the U.S. Post Office to issue a Jack Benny commemorative postage stamp.

Yet in spite of his classic routines and anecdotes, his stories and his jokes, and his best-selling books and record-breaking night club appearances, George Burns always remained a rather private person.

Rarely would he reveal intimacies about himself. His serious side was reserved for talking about comedy, writing, and performing, the elements of his given craft.

His only serious negative press was in December 1938, when on December 13, the lead in *The New York Times* announced that George Burns "Pleads Guilty of Jewel Smuggling." It was the first and only scandal of his career. He and Jack Benny had inadvertently brought some jewelry into the country without the knowledge that they were carrying smuggled goods.

Jack Benny's lawyer, William J. (Wild Bill) Donovan, persuaded Burns to plead guilty. George paid a $10,000 fine and was given a six-month suspended sentence and the matter was finally closed.

"Wild Bill" Donovan, of course, would later become director of the OSS during World War II. The only comment George made during the hearing and beyond was "No comment!" A clear embarrassment, he never broached the matter publicly again.

Of course, in later years he was routinely seen in the company of lovely young women, many of whom could have been a granddaughter. It became part of his routine, and he exploited it for comedic reasons. But he was a gentleman of the old school. He may have joked and laughed, but he never revealed anything truly personal.

We have seen that it was Lisa Miller, never George himself, who made statements about his alleged prowess as a lover.

Similarly, when Larry King asked George in 1989 whether he ever considered marriage after Gracie, George was brief and to the point. He seemed to resent any intrusion into his private life. His answer was brief and terse.

"No way," George replied. "I went around with a little girl, Cathy Carr, in Dallas. She wanted to get married but I was fifty years older than she was. So I told her to get married." A few months earlier he told a friend, "Listen, I'm ninety-two years old. She wants to get married. What am I, crazy?"

Nor did he ever talk frankly about his first marriage, to Hannah Siegal.

George always seemed to downplay his role as straight man to Gracie Allen. The truth simply is that the role of a straight man is a talent all its own. Lou Costello never stopped lauding Bud Abbott. Moreover, in a recent interview Jerry Lewis vehemently insisted that what made the team of Martin and Lewis work so well was not himself, but rather Dean Martin. Lewis was also quick to credit George Burns as the real glue cementing the team of Burns and Allen.

Gracie Allen was an extraordinary talent. To the very end he kept her in the forefront of his life. Even at the height of his new career, he never forgot her and he made sure that no one else ever would. Remarkably, much of his audience during these later years were either very young or had not yet been born when Gracie died in 1964.

Talent is a difficult yardstick to measure. Some may

argue rightfully that George Burns' presence and cha-
risma was sheer talent in itself. To be sure, George knew
comedy, every angle, every aspect. His sense of timing
was impeccable, his delivery and manner unique.

He was not only an actor, he was a darn good actor.
"George was a natural as an actor," insists Carl Reiner,
who directed him in *Oh, God!* "He listened to the other
actor in the scene," a prime requisite for good acting.

But most important, he was a fine human being. And
while he loved his work and was a skilled businessman,
he didn't work solely for the money. By the time of
Gracie's death he was already a wealthy man. By the
mid-1980s he had enough money to donate one million
dollars to Cedars-Sinai Medical Center in Los Angeles,
and a million dollars more to the Motion Picture and
Television Country House and Hospital in Woodland
Hills.

Anytime a waiter, a security guard, or a bellboy would
show him a special courtesy or extend a favor, he would
tell his manager, Irving Fein, to take care of them, then
walk away as Fein peeled bills from a thick roll of cash.

Yet his chief solace was always his work. "You know
you cry and you cry and you cry. And finally there are
no more tears. And then you go back to work," he told
an interviewer in 1989. "Every time you come home
you feel bad . . . because Gracie isn't there." To the
end, George continued to live in the big white Beverly
Hills home they shared, and always kept her tiny little
wedding ring in his pocket on a watch chain.

The eighteenth-century British philosopher Edmund
Burke once said quite aptly that "People will not look
forward to posterity who do not look backward to their
ancestors."

No one person gave more to the world of entertainment in the twentieth century than George Burns: vaudeville, radio, film, television, night clubs, he was there for them all. And he did them all so splendidly. In a world that has often been ugly and bleak, George Burns always gave us a smile, a song, and a warm feeling in our hearts. He was a master craftsman, pure and simple. He was a headliner his whole lifetime. Even in vaudeville he had a star spot, next to closing.

Once when asked what he would like for his own epitaph, he said, "I'd like to be standing there reading it."

Perhaps Winston Churchill might have said it like this as he critiqued show business then and now:

"Never in the twentieth century did one entertainer give so much, to so many, for so long!"

Chances are both George and Gracie would have liked that.

# Sources

*Advertising Age,* March 13, 1993

Blyth, Cheryl, *Say Goodnight, Gracie,* 1986

*Christian Science Monitor,* March 12, 1996

*Cigar Aficionado,* Winter 1994

*Esquire,* December 1975

Fein, Irving, *Jack Benny: An Intimate Biography,* 1976

Gottfried, Martin, *George Burns and the Hundred-Year Dash,* 1996

*Guardian,* August 10, 1975

*Hobbies,* September 1979

*Jack Paar Show,* November 2, 1962, NBC

*Jet,* February 6, 1984

*Ladies' Home Journal,* December 1984

*Larry King Live,* CNN, November 10, 1989

*Life,* May 26, 1972

*Los Angeles Times,* March 10, 1996

*McCall's,* May 1963

*McCall's,* June 1988

*Macleans,* August 20, 1977

*Macleans,* January 29, 1996

*Newsweek,* December 26, 1988

*New York Herald Tribune,* March 8, 1940

*New York Post,* March 11, 1996

*New York Times,* December 13, 1938

*New York Times,* August 29, 1964

*New York Times,* March 10, 1996

*New York Times Magazine,* August 6, 1979

*New York Times Magazine,* June 18, 1989

*New Yorker,* March 15, 1976

*People's Weekly,* October 31, 1988

*Publishers Weekly,* September 28, 1989

Rivers, Joan, *Five Hundredth Show Anniversary,* Tribune Entertainment

*Roy Leonard Show, Interview with George Burns,* Tribune Enterprises/WGN Radio, 1980

*Saturday Evening Post,* May/June 1987

*Saturday Evening Post,* March 1989

*Saturday Evening Post,* April 1990

*Scholastic,* April 19, 1940

*60 Minutes,* Ed Bradley interview, January 6, 1988, CBS

*Stars Salute Israel at 30,* May 8, 1978, ABC

*Time,* December 28, 1938

*Time,* March 18, 1940

*Time,* August 6, 1979

*Tonight Show,* Johnny Carson's 10th Anniversary, September 3, 1972, NBC

*TV Guide,* December 1953

*TV Guide,* September 15, 1954

*TV Guide,* November 6, 1954

*TV Guide,* September 28, 1957

*TV Guide,* October 25, 1958

*Variety,* May 8, 1940

*Variety,* April 26, 1989

*Variety,* May 10, 1989

*Variety,* November 5, 1990

*Video,* July 1989

Wilde, Larry, *The Great Comedians Talk About Comedy,* 1965